THE

FRENCH

DIRECTORY

3rd edition

the complete guide to learning French in France

EUROPA ☆ PAGES

SUMMERSDALE

Summersdale Publishers
46 West Street
Chichester
West Sussex
PO19 1RP
England

Email: summersdale@summersdale.com

Published in association with:
Europa Pages
PO Box 1369
Ascot
Berks.
SL5 7YH
England

E-Mail: france@europa-pages.co.uk

ISBN 1 84024 049 0

A CIP catalogue record for this book is available from the
British Library.

Printed and bound in Great Britain by
Biddles Ltd, Guildford and King's Lynn.

Note:
Whilst every effort has been made to ensure the accuracy of all information
contained in this directory, neither Europa Pages nor Summersdale Publishers
can accept any liability for any loss or damage resulting from omissions or
inaccuracies, relating to telephone numbers, addresses, wording, spacing, or
positioning of any listing, advertisement or other material, regardless of how caused.

CONTENTS

Introduction

LEARNING FRENCH IN FRANCE

French is the mother tongue of some 200 million people around the world. It is an official language in Belgium, Canada, Luxembourg and Switzerland, as well as a host of African countries including Zaire and Niger.

To a great extent, French is still seen as *the* language of diplomacy, both in the European Union and on an international level.

Whilst it is possible to acquire a good level of French from tuition in your own country, only a stay in a French speaking environment will give your French an authentic feel and ensure rapid progress.

In France, the language learning process does not stop the minute you leave the classroom, but continues throughout the day. Buying lunch, shopping, finding your way around : all involve language practice with native speakers.

You will find studying French in France both a fun and rewarding experience: a million miles away from those tedious school lessons trying to learn your irregular verbs!

It is possible to combine a language course with a holiday; indeed, many schools offer a range of sports and activities enabling you to have the best of both worlds.

HOW TO USE THIS BOOK

In this book, France is divided into 7 geographic regions (see map on page 15).

1.   Paris and the Ile-de-France
2.   Northern France
3.   Eastern France
4.   South-East France
5.   South-West France
6.   Western France
7.   Central France

Each region is preceded by an introduction to the area and some of its sights, in order to give readers a *flavour* of some of the attractions on offer. Details of low-cost accommodation are then supplied, in addition to the addresses of national bed and breakfast agencies given at beginning of the book.

The A-Z listing of courses contains the name and addresses of each school plus information on prices, exam preparation, number of study hours per week etc..

Please note that the information contained in this book was supplied to us in good faith. We do not recommend any one particular school, and advise readers to write off to *several* institutions, in order to obtain further information about the courses on offer.

(A sample letter in French is shown on the next page to help you, although most schools would be able to understand English.)

Sample Letter to Schools

(Your Name & Address)

Messieurs,   *(date)*

Ayant vu l' annonce pour votre école dans Europa Pages' French Directory, j'aimerais recevoir de plus amples renseignements sur vos cours de français.

Mes co-ordonnées:

J'aimerais faire mon stage du _____(date) au _____(date).

J'étudie le français depuis _____

Age_____ Nationalité_____

Dans l'attente de votre réponse, je vous prie d'agréer, Messieurs, mes salutations distinguées.

(Your name and signature)

 ## Telephoning or Faxing France from Abroad:

Dial the international access code (+33) then the area code *minus the 0* followed by the actual number.

e.g. a Paris number 01 12 34 56 78 becomes:
 +33 1 12 34 56 78

ESSENTIAL INFORMATION

 ## VISAS & PAPERS

British and Irish travellers (as members of the European Union) are in an enviable position; they do not require visas and more importantly they can work in France without any difficulties.

The situation for non-EU members is a bit different. Whilst Americans, Canadians and New Zealanders do not need a visa to enter the country, they will find it hard to obtain a work permit. However, if you are going to be studying in France, you can apply for a student visa. This entitles the bearer to work on a part-time basis, but it must be applied for *before* entering France.

For all matters concerning visas and work permits, contact your nearest French embassy or consulate:

 ## FRENCH EMBASSIES AND CONSULATES

AUSTRALIA
Embassy: 6, Perth avenue, Yarralumla A.C.T. 2600.
TEL : (06) 2705111. FAX : (06) 2733193.
Consulate: 492 St Kilda Rd, Melbourne, Victoria 3004.
TEL : (03) 98200921 FAX : (03) 98209363.
General Consulate: Level 26, St-Martins Tower,
31, Market St.,Sydney N.S.W. 2000.
TEL : (02) 92625779. FAX : (02) 92831210.

CANADA
Embassy: 42, Promenade Sussex, Ottawa, ONT. K1M 2C9.
TEL : (613) 7891795. FAX : (613) 7890279.
General Consulate: 250, Lutz St. C.P. 1109,
Moncton N.B. E1C 8P6.
TEL : (506) 8574191 FAX : (506) 8588169.
General Consulate: 1, Place Ville-Marie, 26th floor,
bureau 2601 Montreal H3B 4S3.
TEL : (514) 8784385 FAX : (514) 8783981.
General Consulate: 25, rue Saint-Louis Quebec QC G1R 3Y8.

TEL : (418) 6880430. FAX : (418) 6942297.
General Consulate: 130, Bloor St. West, Suite 400
Toronto-Ont. M5S 1N5.
TEL : (416) 9258041 FAX : (416) 9253076.
General Consulate: 1201-736 Granville St.,
Vancouver B.C. V6Z 1H9.
TEL : (604) 6814345. FAX : (604) 6814287.

IRELAND
Embassy: 36, Ailesbury Rd, Ballsbridge, Dublin 4.
TEL : (01) 2601666. FAX : (01) 2830178.

NEW ZEALAND
Embassy: 1, Willeston St., P.O. box 1695. Wellington
TEL : (04) 4720200. FAX : (04) 4725887.

SOUTH AFRICA
Embassy (Jan-June): 1009 Main Tower,
Cape Town Center, Heerengracht, 8001 Cape Town.
TEL : (021) 212050 FAX : (032) 261996.
Embassy (July-Dec): 807, George avenue, Arcadia, Pretoria 0083.
TEL : (012) 435564 FAX : (012) 433481.
General Consulate: Carlton Center, 35th floor Commissioner St.
P.O. box 11278, Johannesburg 2000.
TEL : (011) 3313460 FAX : (011) 3313497.
Consulate: 2, Dean St., Gardens, 8001 Cape Town
TEL : (021) 231575 FAX : (021) 248470.

UNITED KINGDOM
Embassy: 58 Knightsbridge, London SW1X 7JT
TEL: (0171) 201 1000 FAX: (0171) 201 1053
Consulate: 21 Cromwell Road, London SW7 2EN
TEL: (0171) 838 2000 FAX: (0171) 838 2001
11 Randolph Crescent, Edinburgh EH3 7TT
TEL: (0131) 225 7954 FAX: (0131) 225 8975

UNITED STATES
Embassy: 4101 Reservoir Rd N.W. Washington D.C. 20007
TEL : (202) 9446000. FAX : (202) 9446166
General Consulate: 4101 Reservoir Rd N.W. Washington D.C.
20007. TEL : (202) 9446195. FAX : (202) 9446148.
General Consulate: 285, Peachtree center avenue, suite 2800,
Marquis Two Tower. Atlanta, GA 30303.
TEL : (404) 5224226. FAX : (404) 8809408.

General Consulate: Park Square Building, suite 750,
31 Saint James avenue, Boston MA 02116.
TEL : (617) 5427374. FAX : (617) 5428054.
General Consulate: 737, North Michigan avenue. Olympia Center,
suite 2020. Chicago-IL 60611.
TEL : (312) 7875359 FAX : (312) 6644196.
General Consulate: 2777 Allen Parkway, Riviana Building,
suite 650. Houston, TX 77019.
TEL : (713) 5282181. FAX : (713) 5281933.
General Consulate: Lykes center - 300 Poyras, suite 2105.
New Orleans, LA 70130.
TEL : (504) 5235772 FAX : (504) 5235725.
General Consulate: 10990, Wilshire boulevard, suite 300.
Los Angeles, CA 90024.
TEL : (310) 2353200. FAX : (310) 3120704.
General Consulate: 1, Biscayne Tower, suite 1710,
2 South Biscayne blvd. Miami, FL 33131.
TEL : (305) 3729799. FAX : (305) 3729549.
General Consulate: 934, Fifth Avenue. New York, NY 10021.
TEL : (212) 6063600 FAX : (212) 6063620.
General Consulate: 540, Bush St.. San Francisco, CA 94108.
TEL : (415) 3974330. FAX : (415) 4338357.

ONCE IN FRANCE

 TELEPHONES

In October 1996, a new ten digit system was introduced in
France. The country is now divided into five zones, each
one taking the following area code:

>   01 Paris and the Ile-de-France
>   02 North West
>   03 North East
>   04 South East
>   05 South West

When dialling within France, you must use the new area
codes.

To dial abroad from France:

Dial 00 + your country code, then the area code minus the 0 and the number.
> e.g. a London number 0171 123 4567 becomes:
> 00 44 171 123 4567

Cheap Rates:

50% discounts are available:
7pm to 8am Monday to Friday.
12.00pm Saturday to 8am Monday.

0800 numbers are free.

Telephone Boxes:

Watch out, as very few take coins. You will need to buy a *télécarte*, available from post offices, newsagents, some bars, tobacconists and métro stations.
Price: 50 units = 40.60 FF   120 units = 97.50 FF.

Emergency Numbers:

Police: 17
Ambulance: 15
Fire: 18
Operator: 13
Directory Enquires: 12

Lost or stolen credit cards:

Visa: 08 36 69 08 80
Mastercard - Eurocard: 01 45 67 84 84
American Express: 01 47 77 72 00
Diner's Club: 01 47 77 72 00

RECEIVING MAIL

If you don't have a permanent address in France, mail can be sent to your nearest post office.

Mail should be addressed as follows:

YOUR SURNAME IN CAPITALS, First Name in small case
Poste Restante
(Address of your local post office)
Area Code, Town, FRANCE

If you want the mail sent to the main post office, add the words 'Recette Principale' after Poste Restante.

NB: Take some ID (passport, national ID card) each time you go to collect your mail. A small handling charge will be levied.

 OPENING HOURS:

Post Offices: 8am to 7pm weekdays.
8am to noon Saturdays.
Closed on Sundays.

Banks: 9am to noon & 2pm to 4 pm weekdays.
Closed either on a Saturday or Monday.
(Most banks in Paris do not close for lunch.)

Food Shops: 7am to 6.30pm or 7.30pm
Some open Sunday mornings.
Hypermarkets usually open from 9am to 10pm, Mon-Sat.

Other Shops: 9am or 10am to 6.30pm or 7.30 pm
Many close on Mondays and shops in the provinces
often close for lunch (noon to 2pm).

STUDENT & YOUTH CARDS:

International Student Identity Card (*la carte d'étudiant internationale*)

Available to students in full-time higher education. Entitles bearer to a wide range of reductions and allows use of university canteens (resto U). Costs 60 FF in France, and is available from various travel agents or CROUS and CNOUS centres.

Carte Jeune Internationale 'Go 25'

Available to the under 25s. Allows bearer cheaper travel rates, sports etc. Costs 45 FF and can be purchased at OTU Voyage travel agencies around France.

Carte Jeunes

For those under 26 years old. Allows a range of discounts in France and 20 other European countries. Costs 120 FF and can be bought at train stations and CRIJ centres throughout France.
Website: http://www.cartejeunes.fr

NB: It is worth while taking some passport photos with you to France, which should be cut to size (as you'll never be able to find scissors when you want them!). They are needed for student ID cards, for rail/ métro passes (like the 'carte orange' for the Paris métro) and are often required by the school for their registration forms.

CONSULATES IN PARIS

Australia: 4, rue Jean Rey, 75015 Paris. TEL: (01) 45 79 80 44

Canada: 35, avenue Montaigne, 75008 Paris. TEL: (01) 44 43 29 00

Ireland: 4, rue Rude, 75116 Paris. TEL: (01) 45 00 20 87

New Zealand: 7ter, rue Léonard de Vinci, 75116 Paris
TEL: (01) 45 00 24 11

South Africa: 59, quai d'Orsay, 75007 Paris. TEL: (01) 45 55 92 37

United Kingdom: 16, rue d' Anjou, 75008 Paris.TEL:(01) 42 66 38 10

United States: 2, rue Saint Florentin, 75001 Paris. TEL: (01) 42 96 12 02

 BUDGET ACCOMMODATION

'En-Famille'

Staying with a French family is a good way of improving your language skills and provides a useful introduction to the French way of life.

Most language schools have a placement service, and can put you in touch with families in their area. If your school does not run this type of service, you could contact one of the organisations below, which specialise in finding French families for young foreigners.

Accueil Familial des Jeunes Etrangers
23, rue Cherche-Midi, 75006 Paris
TEL: (01) 42 22 50 34 FAX: (01) 45 44 60 48

Amicale Culturelle Internationale
27, rue Godot-de-Mauroy, 75009 Paris
TEL: (01) 47 42 94 21 FAX: (01) 49 24 02 67

Goelangues
33, rue de Trévise, 75009 Paris
TEL: (01) 45 23 39 39 FAX: (01) 45 23 39 23

Inter-Séjour
179, rue de Courcelles, 75017 Paris
TEL: (01) 47 63 06 81 FAX: (01) 40 54 89 41

Vacances Jeunes
88, rue de Miromesnil, 75008 Paris
TEL: (01) 42 89 39 39 FAX: (01) 43 59 08 34

Bed & Breakfast

There are numerous organisations which place visitors
in private homes throughout France. All offer breakfast,
and some can provide other meals as well. Below are
the details of a few of these organisations, but remember
that some have a compulsory membership fee, which
only pays for itself if you intend to stay for a while.

Accueil France Famille
5, rue François Coppée, 75015 Paris
TEL: (01) 45 54 22 39 FAX: (01) 45 58 43 25

France Accueil Contacts
3, rue du Colonel Moll, 75017 Paris
TEL: (01) 47 42 57 94 FAX: (01) 42 68 15 29

France Lodge
5, rue Faubourg Montmartre, 75009 Paris.
TEL: (01) 42 46 68 19 FAX: (01) 42 46 65 61

International Café Couette
8, rue d'Isly, 75008 Paris
TEL: (01) 42 94 92 00 FAX: (01) 42 94 93 12

MAP OF FRENCH REGIONS

KEY TO REGIONS:

1. Paris and the Ile-de-France
2. Northern France
3. Eastern France
4. South-East France
5. South-West France
6. Western France
7. Central France

1 PARIS
& THE ILE-DE-FRANCE

Paris, a city which needs little introduction, it is known the world over for its romantic atmosphere, beautiful boulevards and elegant buildings.

Take a trip down the Seine in the Bateaux Mouches and enjoy a scenic view of Notre Dame and the Eiffel Tower.

Visit some of the finest museums in the world: the Louvre, with its stunning glass pyramid, contains a vast collection of treasures including, of course, the Mona Lisa. Nearby, the Musée D' Orsay, a converted train station, is a perfect setting for an outstanding display of impressionist paintings, with works by Van Gogh, Cézanne, Renoir and virtually every well known artist of that time. The eye-catching Pompidou Centre houses modern art, whilst the Musée Picasso is a must for devotees of this artist.

For fashion conscious visitors, the large department stores and hundreds of boutiques offer an endless choice of clothes and accessories.

In the evenings the cafés and restaurants cater for all tastes, whilst clubs and cabarets stay open until the small hours.

Only 25 minutes from Paris is Versailles. The splendid château, with its stunning gardens, fountains and the famous 'Hall of Mirrors' are not to be missed.

Fontainebleau, also a short distance from Paris, dates back to the 12th century. It is particularly known for its *Cours des Adieux* where Napoleon bid farewell to his Imperial Guards. The forest of Fontainebleau spreads over 50,000 acres, attracting many climbers because of its huge rock formations.

AVERAGE TEMPERATURES FOR PARIS (° C):

Jan / Mar	Apr / Jun	Jul / Sep	Oct / Dec
7.5 / 10	16 / 23	25 / 21	16.5 / 8

 LOW COST ACCOMMODATION:

During the summer it is possible for students and young people to stay in university residences.
Prices shown are per person per night and include breakfast - lowest prices are for a room with 4 beds, most expensive are for an individual room.

BVJ Paris/ Opéra
11 rue Thérèse, 75001 Paris
TEL: (01) 42 60 77 23   Price: 120 FF

BVJ Paris/ Louvre
20 rue Jean-Jacques Rousseau, 75001 Paris
TEL: (01) 42 36 88 18   Price: 120 FF

BVJ Paris/ Les Halles
5 rue du pélican, 75001 Paris
TEL: (01) 40 26 92 45   Price: 120 FF

AJF Beaubourg
119 rue St. Martin, 75004 Paris
TEL: (01) 42 77 87 80   Price: 113 FF + 10 FF reservation

AJF Marais
16 rue du Pont Louis-Philippe, 75004 Paris
TEL: (01) 42 77 87 80   Price: 113 FF + 10 FF reservation

\AJF Quartier Latin
139 Bd. St. Michel, 75005 Paris
TEL: (01) 43 54 95 86   Price: 113 FF + 10 FF reservation

BVJ Paris/ Quartier Latin
44 rue des Bernardins, 75005 Paris
TEL: (01) 43 29 34 80   Price:120 FF

Association des Etudiants Protestants
46 rue Vaugirard, 75006 Paris
TEL: (01) 43 54 31 49   Price: 75 FF (2040 FF per month)

AJF Gare du Nord
Pass.4 - 4, rue du Dunkerque, 75009 Paris
TEL: (01) 42 85 86 19   Price: 113 FF + 10 FF reservation

Maison Internationale des Jeunes
4 rue Titon, 75011 Paris
TEL: (01) 43 71 99 21   Price: 110 FF

CISP Maurice Ravel
6 av. Maurice Ravel, 75012 Paris
TEL: (01) 44 75 60 00   Price: 127 FF to 145 FF

CISP Kellermann
17 Bd. Kellermann, 75013 Paris
TEL: (01) 44 16 37 38   Price: 127 FF to 145 FF

Maison des Clubs UNESCO
43 rue de la glacière, 75013 Paris
TEL: (01) 43 36 00 63   Price: 111 FF to 151 FF

FIAP - Jean Monnet
30 rue Cabanis, 75014 Paris
TEL: (01) 45 89 89 15   Price: 146 FF to 251 FF

Auberge de Jeunesse 'LE D'ARTAGNAN'
80 rue Vitruve, 75020 Paris
TEL: (01) 40 32 34 56   Price: 106 FF to 126 FF

CAAP
46 rue Louis Lumière, 75020 Paris
TEL: (01) 43 61 24 51   Price: 100 FF to 138 FF

If you want to rent a studio or share an apartment with others,
a good source of information is the American Church (65 Quai
d' Orsay in the 7th arrondissement). The notice board there
contains a host of rooms for rent and flat shares, but be warned:
it is always extremely busy, and the good deals go fast.

A ➡ Z   DIRECTORY OF COURSES IN THIS REGION

Accord - Ecole de Langues
52 rue Montmartre, 75002 Paris
Tel: 01 42 36 24 95 Fax: 01 42 21 17 91
Email: accordel@easynet.fr
Web: http://www.accord-langues.com

Hours/wk: 6-28
Price/wk (FF): 270-2900
Class size: 14 (10 average)
Min. stay: 1 week
Min. age: 18 (15 summer)
Open: All year

Exams: DELF / DALF, CCIP

Accommodation: Families, residences, foyers, studios or hotels.

Special courses: French for business / commerce. Courses for teachers.

Other useful points: Au pair programmes (6,9,12hrs/wk), 'Junior Club' for 15-18 yrs in the summer costs 3000FF/wk all inclusive.

Alliance Française de Paris
101 boulevard Raspail
75270 Paris Cedex 06
Tel: 01 45 44 38 28 Fax: 01 45 44 89 42
Email: info@paris.alliancefrancaise.fr
Web:http://www.paris.alliancefrancaise.fr

Hours/wk: 6-20
Price (FF): 1340/mth-4020/mth
Class size: 16-22
Min. stay: 2 weeks
Min. age: 16
Open: All year

Exams: DELF/ DALF, CCIP & Alliance Française

Accommodation: Families

Special courses: French for business, tourism, law, secretaries. Courses for teachers.

Other useful points: Many facilities including library, self-service language laboratory and cinema club. Also a useful notice board for students with job offers, rooms for rent etc.

American Dream Center
163 rue de Charenton
75012 Paris
Tel: 01 43 42 26 00
Fax: 01 43 42 12 00

Hours/wk: 4-10
Price/wk (FF): On application
Class size: 1-8
Min. stay: 1 week
Min. age: 16
Open: All year

Other useful points:
Also runs English courses for French speakers.

Assist Langues
23 rue Pradier
75019 Paris
Tel: 01 42 03 23 23
Fax: 01 42 03 36 14

Hours/wk: 15-20
Price/wk (FF): 1200-1800
Class size: 4-5
Min. stay: 2 weeks
Min. age: 18
Open: All year except July / Aug + school holidays

Accommodation: Hotels

Special courses: On demand. Also tailor-made courses (business, tourism, telephone skills)

Other useful points: Excursion guides available.

Berlitz
35, avenue Franklin Roosevelt
75008 Paris
Tel: 01 40 74 00 17
Fax: 01 45 61 49 79
Email: berlitzcrochard@minitel.fr
Web: http://www.berlitz.com

Hours/wk: 15
Price (FF): 120/hr
Class size: 1-1 (or very small groups)
Min. stay: 1 week
Open: All year

Exams: DELF / DALF, CCIP

Accommodation: Families, youth hostels or hotels.

Special courses: Commercial French

Other useful points: Start any Monday. Conversation club arranges meetings with French speakers.

Berlitz (Main centre)
38, avenue de l'Opéra
75002 Paris
Tel: 01 44 94 50 00
Fax: 01 44 94 50 05
Web: http://www.berlitz.com

Berlitz offers 1-1 tuition all year, including evening courses and Saturday mornings.

Group tuition is available June to August only.

Several centres in Paris including:

15, place de la Nation
75011 Paris
Tel: 01 43 73 28 47 Fax: 01 43 73 26 37

31, rue du Sommerard
75005 Paris
Tel: 01 46 33 98 77 Fax: 01 46 33 92 14

23, avenue Victor Hugo
75016 Paris
Tel: 01 45 00 08 68 Fax: 01 45 01 63 97

CEI/ Club des 4 Vents
BP 5
75660 Paris cedex 14
Tel: 01 45 65 95 21
Fax: 01 45 65 95 30
Email: CEI_4Vents@compuserve.com

Hours/wk: 15-20
Price (FF): from 5150/2wks
Min. stay: 2 weeks
Min. age: 16
Open: Summer

Accommodation: Families or residences (included in the price).

Special courses: Parisian architecture, history of French fashion, cookery courses.

Other useful points: 8 locations around France. Activities, sports and cultural visits in the afternoons. Also has a school in Paris (see Paris Langues)

Centre International d'Etudes Pédagogiques (CIEP)
1 avenue Léon-Journault
BP 75
92318 Sèvres Cedex
Tel: 01 45 07 60 00
Fax: 01 45 07 60 01
Email: virollet@ciep.fr
Web: http://www.ciep.fr

No pre-set courses. Tuition is arranged to meet the needs of individual companies or institutions.

Special courses: Wide range of courses for teachers of FLE (over 80 each year). Contact the centre for full details.

Cetradel
120 avenue des Champs Elysées
75008 Paris
Tel: 01 56 69 21 00
Fax: 01 56 69 21 01
Email: cetradel@wanadoo.fr
Web: http://www.cetradel-france-langue.com

Hours/wk: 15-30
Price/wk (FF): 2200-12,600
Class size: 1-6
Min. stay: 1 week
Min. age: 18
Open: All year

Accommodation: Families, residences or hotels.

Special courses: French for business, tourism, telecommunications, human resources and finance.

Other useful points: Immersion programmes: 'language & culture'. Multimedia facilities.

Citylangues
52, 54 rue de Capitaine Guynemer
92400 Courbevoie - Paris - La Défense 6
Tel: 01 47 89 38 05
Fax: 01 49 05 40 47
Email: citylangues@wanadoo.fr
Web: http://www.citylangues.com

Hours/wk: 20-40
Price/wk (FF): 7700-15400
Class size: 1-5
Min. stay: 1 week
Min. age: 18
Open: All year

Exams: On demand

Accommodation: Families or hotels.

Special courses: Tailor-made on request

Other useful points: Intensive executive courses only.

Chambre de Commerce et d'Industrie de Paris (CCIP)
DRI, 28 rue de l'Abbé-Grégoire
75279 Paris Cedex 06
Tel: 01 49 54 28 74
Fax: 01 49 54 28 90
Email: examdfda@ccip.fr
Web: http://www.fda.ccip.fr

Hours/wk: 6-35
Price (FF): 5000 (semester at 6hrs/wk)
Min. stay: 1 week
Min. age: 18
Open: All year

Exams: CCIP and TEF

Accommodation: You're provided with a list of foyers and hotels.

Special courses: Business French and courses for teachers.

Other useful points: Open to business professionals or company groups. Training courses outside France can be arranged for universities or companies.

Cours de Langues et Civilisation Françaises de la Sorbonne
47 rue des Ecoles
75005 Paris
Tel: 01 40 46 26 64
Fax: 01 40 46 32 29
Web: http://www.fle.fr/sorbonne

Hours/wk: 6-25
Price (FF): 3500-11900 (semester)
Class size: 25
Min. stay: 1 mth (summer), 1 semester (all other times of year)
Min. age: 18 (with equivalent of baccalaureate)
Open: All year

Exams: CCIP + Sorbonne's own

Special courses: French for business. Courses for teachers.

Other useful points: Summer courses (June-Sept) lasting min. 4wks cost from 2200/mth.

Demos Langues
20, rue de l'Arcade
75008 Paris
Tel: 01 44 94 16 31
Fax: 01 44 94 16 35
Email: langues@demos.fr
Web: http://www.demos.fr

Hours/wk: ½-40
Price/wk (FF): On application
Class size: 1-6
Min. stay: 10 hours
Min. age: 11
Open: All year

Special courses: French for business. Business life in France.

Other useful points: Part of 'Groupe Demos' which has over 25 years experience in business training.

Ecole de Langue Française pour Etrangers (ELFE)
8 Villa Ballu, 75009 Paris
Tel: 01 48 78 73 00 Fax: 01 40 82 91 92
Email: contact@elfe-paris.com
Web: http://www.elfe-paris.com

Hours/wk: 15-23
Price/wk (FF): 2250-3750
Class size: 6 max
Min. stay: 2 weeks (see below)
Min. age: 18
Open: All year

Exams: DELF / DALF, CCIP

Accommodation: Families, residences or hotels

Special courses: French for business. 'Grande Ecole' preparation. Courses for teachers.

Other useful points: Intensive courses lasting 1wk min. offered (15hrs in group + 10 hrs 1-1 tuition = 6000FF/wk) Cookery courses (at the Ritz hotel) also organised.

EAP International Executive Centre
6 av. de la Porte de Champerret
75838 Paris cedex 17
Tel: 01 44 09 33 12
Fax: 01 44 09 35 34
Email: sbregeon@eap.net
Web: http://www.eap.net

Hours/wk: 18-36
Price/wk (FF): 6900-13800
Class size: 2-4
Min. stay: 1 week
Min. age: 19
Open: 5 Jan-31 July, 1 Oct-20 Dec

Exams: CCIP, Alliance Française

Accommodation: Residence or hotels

Special courses: French for business, management, law etc.

Other useful points: Internships and study abroad programmes at EAP Paris for foreign students.

Ecole Eiffel
3, rue Crocé-Spinelli
75014 Paris
Tel: 01 43 20 37 41
Fax: 01 43 20 49 13
Email: eiffelfr@club-internet.fr
http://www.ccip.fr/club/75/ecole-eiffel.html

Hours/wk: 3½ - 20
Price/wk (FF): 300-700
Class size: 6-12
Min. stay: 2 weeks
Min. age: 16 (14 during holidays)
Open: All year

Exams: DELF / DALF preparation

Accommodation: Families, university residences, studios, apartments, hotels.

Special courses: Commercial French. Medical French. Literature & civilisation.

Other useful points: Cultural excursions are arranged.

Ecole Européenne de Gestion
169 Quai de Valmy
75010 Paris
Tel: 01 53 35 84 84
Fax: 01 53 35 84 92

Hours/wk: 25
Price/wk (FF): 1500
Class size: small groups
Min. stay: 1 month
Min. age: 18
Open: All year

Exams: CCIP

Accommodation: Contact their accommodation service for details.

Special courses: French for business

Other useful points: Intensive summer courses run in July and August (preparing for the Certificat Pratique - CCIP). During the year non-intensive courses for the Cert.Prat. and the Dip. Supérieur.

Ecole Internationale de l'Accueil Franco-Nordique
28 rue Vignon
75009 Paris
Tel: 01 42 66 53 02
Fax: 01 42 66 53 32

Hours/wk: 6-20
Price/wk (FF): 500 (10rs/wk - summer)
Class size: 15 max
Min. stay: 1 week (summer)
Min. age: 18 (16 summer)
Open: All year

Exams: DELF

Accommodation: Families, foyers or hotels

Special courses: Courses for teachers

Other useful points: Au-pair placement service (for stays of 9-12mths). Excursions, guided visits and social evenings arranged.

Ecole Suisse Internationale de Français Appliqué
10 rue des messageries
75010 Paris
Tel: 01 47 70 20 66
Fax: 01 42 46 34 57

Hours/wk: 25-30
Price/wk (FF): 1710
Class size: 5-15
Min. stay: 1 week
Min. age: 16
Open: All year

Exams: DELF, CCIP

Accommodation: Families, studios or hotels.

Special courses: French for business. Courses for teachers.

Other useful points: Translation courses (German/French). Library, computer & video room, language laboratory. Visits and social evenings.

EF Corporate
3 rue de Bassano
75116 Paris
Tel: 01 47 20 18 02
Fax: 01 47 20 18 80
Web: http://www.ef.com

Hours/wk: 40
Price/wk (FF): On application
Class size: 1-1 tuition
Min. stay: 1 week
Min. age: 18

Special courses: Conversational business and social French.

Other useful points: Intensive executive courses only, for all levels. The centre has a language laboratory and small coffee lounge. Excursions are organised.

EF Education (French Head Office)
4 rue Duphot
75001 Paris
Tel: 01 42 61 50 22
Fax: 01 42 61 75 44
Web: http://www.ef.com

Hours/wk: 20-30
Price: 1240 US$/2wks
Class size: 12 average (15 summer)
Min. stay: 2 weeks
Open: All year

Accommodation: Full-board accommodation with families is included in the price. Alternatively, students can stay at the EF residence, about 30mins from the school.

Other useful points: The school is within walking distance of the Louvre museum and Notre Dame. Airport transfers can be arranged (extra charge).

Executive Language Services (ELS)
20 rue Sainte-Croix de la Bretonnerie
75004 Paris
Tel: 01 44 54 58 88
Fax: 01 48 04 55 53
Email: els@club-internet.fr

ELS runs general language, business and executive courses.

Contact them for more details.

Eurocentre
13 passage Dauphine
75006 Paris
Tel: 01 40 46 72 00
Fax: 01 40 46 72 06
Email: par-info@eurocentres.com
Web: http://www.eurocentres.com

Hours/wk: 25
Price/wk (FF): 1073-3000 (approx.)
Class size: 10-15
Min. stay: 2 weeks
Min. age: 16
Open: All year

Exams: DELF, CCIP

Accommodation: Families or hotels

Special courses: French for business. Courses for teachers.

Other useful points: Facilities include audio/video support and computers. Conferences and guided visits arranged.

Formalangues
87 rue la Boetie
75008 Paris
Tel: 01 53 93 67 89
Fax: 01 53 93 67 80
Email: formalangue@wanadoo.fr

Hours/wk: 3-7
Price/wk (FF): 2250-12,000
Class size: 1-6
Min. stay: 1 week
Min. age: 18-80
Open: All year

Exams: DELF / DALF, CCIP

Accommodation: Families, foyers, residences or studios.

Special courses: French for business. Courses for teachers.

Other useful points: Video and multimedia facilities.

**Formation Postuniversitaire
Internationale**
11 rue Tiquetonne
75002 Paris
Tel: 01 40 28 04 03
Fax: 01 40 28 49 22
Email: fpi@cilf.org
Web: http://www.cilf.org

Hours/wk: 6-12½
Price/wk (FF): 288-463 (approx.)
Min. stay: 1 week
Min. age: 16
Open: All year

Accommodation: Families, foyers or hotels

Special courses: Courses for teachers

Other useful points: Video room and language laboratory. Monthly theatre visit.

IELP
95 bd de Sébastopol
75002 Paris
Tel: 01 42 33 35 84
Fax: 01 42 21 04 66

Hours/wk: 30-40
Price/wk (FF): 12,000-16,000
Class size: 6
Min. stay: 30 hours
Min. age: 18
Open: All year

Accommodation: Can be arranged for you. Various options. Contact school for details.

Special courses: All subjects on request.

Other useful points: Intensive courses aimed at the business market.

France Langue
14 rue Léonard de Vinci
75116 Paris
Tel: 01 45 00 40 15
Fax: 01 45 00 53 41
Email: frlang_p@club-internet.fr
Web: http://www.France-Langue.fr

Hours/wk: 6-30
Price/wk (FF): From 700/wk for 15hrs
Class size: 8-12
Min. stay: 1 week
Min. age: 17
Open: All year

Exams: DELF / DALF, CCIP

Accommodation: Families, residences or hotels.

Special courses: French for business. Courses for teachers.

Other useful points: 1-1 tuition also offered, price 360FF/hr. Self-service mediatheque, with computers, video and language laboratory. Weekly social evening.

Inlingua - La Défense
CNIT, BP 451
2 place de la Défense
92053 Paris La Défense
Tel: 01 46 92 25 70
Fax: 01 46 92 25 68
Web: http://www.inlingua-paris.com

Hours/wk: 3-40
Price/wk (FF): 10,920 + tax (30 hrs)
Class size: 1-1 tuition
Min. stay: Variable
Open: All year

Accommodation: Families (1800FF wk + 1 meal / day) or hotels.

Special courses: French for business and commerce.

Other useful points: Lessons by telephone and tailor-made courses.

Inlingua has two other centres in Paris, offering the same courses as the one shown above (see next page).

Inlingua - Rive Gauche
Esplanade des Invalides
109 rue de l'Université
75007 Paris
Tel: 01 45 51 46 60
Fax: 01 47 05 66 05

Inlingua - Bastille
28, bd Bastille
75012 Paris
Tel: 01 53 17 07 77
Fax: 01 53 17 07 08

(see previous entry for details)

**Institut Catholique de Paris,
Cours Universitaires d'Eté**
21 rue d'Assas
75270 Paris Cedex 06
Tel: 01 44 39 52 58
Fax: 01 45 44 39 52 09
Email: ilcf@icp.fr
Web: http://www.icp.fr

Hours/wk: 20
Price (FF): 3500 / month
Class size: 12-25
Min. stay: 1 month (July)
Min. age: 18
Open: July

Exams: CCIP

Accommodation: Foyer

Special courses: French for business.
Methodology and pedagogy of FLE (for teachers)

Other useful points: Organised excursions and conferences.

Institut Britannique de Paris
Dépt. d'Etudes Françaises
9- 11 rue de Constantine
75340 Paris Cedex 07
Tel: 01 44 11 73 83
Fax: 01 45 50 31 55
Email: campos@ext.jussieu.fr
Web: http://www.bip.lon.ac.uk

Hours/wk: 3
Price (FF): 6000 (term)
Min. stay: 1 term
Min. age: 18
Open: Oct-June

Exams: CCIP

Accommodation: Residences, foyers or studios

Special courses: French for business, history of art.

Other useful points: 3 year BA (Hons) course in French Studies, also MA in Contemporary French Studies.

Institut de Langue et de Culture Françaises (ICP)
21 rue d'Assas
75270 Paris Cedex 06
Tel: 01 44 39 52 68
Fax: 01 44 39 52 09
Email: ilcf@icp.fr
Web: http://www.icp.fr

Hours/wk: 3-30
Price (FF): 42 per hour
Class size: 12-25
Min. stay: 1 semester (or 1mth in Sept)
Min. age: 18
Open: 1st Sept-15th Aug

Exams: CCIP

Accommodation: International Foyer

Special courses: French for business, courses for teachers, contemporary studies.

Other useful points: The Institut Catholique de Paris has a library and arranges conferences and social events.

Institut de Langue Française
3 avenue Bertie-Albrecht, 75008 Paris
Tel: 01 45 63 24 00 Fax: 01 45 63 07 09
Email: ILF@inst-langue-fr.com
Web: http://www.inst-langue-fr.com

Hours/wk: 6-20
Price/wk (FF): 200-800
Class size: 15
Min. stay: 60 mins
Min. age: 18
Open: All year

Exams: DELF / DALF, CCIP
+ ILF - Sorbonne

Accommodation: Families, foyers, residence, studios, apartments or hotels.

Special courses: French for business, French for secretaries

Other useful points: Literature, phonetics and civilisation courses. Cultural activities (e.g. museum visits, tours of Paris). Library.

Institut Parisien
87, Blvd de Grenelle, 75015 Paris
Tel: 01 40 56 09 53 Fax: 01 43 06 46 30
Email: institut.parisien@dial.oleane.com

Hours/wk: 10-25
Price/wk (FF): 620-1750
Class size: 1-12
Min. stay: 1 week
Min. age: 17
Open: All year except Christmas

Exams: CCIP & Sorbonne

Accommodation: Families, foyers or hotels.

Special courses: French for business, for tourism and the hotel trade. French literature, fashion and gastronomy courses.

Other useful points: Courses start each week. Students at the Institut benefit from 1½ hrs of free conferences on French civilisation per week. There is also a special programme for au-pairs.

Institut International de Rambouillet
Le Vieux Moulin, 48-50 rue G. Lenôtre
78120 Rambouillet
Tel: 01 30 46 53 21
Fax: 01 30 46 53 13
Email: iir@easynet.fr
Web: http://www.wp.com/iir

Hours/wk: 15-30
Price (FF): from 1500/mth (see below)
Class size: 10-15
Min. stay: 2 weeks
Min. age: 18
Open: All year

Exams: DELF / DALF

Accommodation: Families or institut's own residence

Special courses: French for business, hotels/restaurants, diplomats, culture/tradition. Courses for teachers.

Other useful points: Tuition + accommodation packages: 2400FF/wk with 30 hrs courses, or 6500FF/mth.

Institute of Applied Language Studies
41 rue de Turenne
75003 Paris
Tel: 01 44 59 25 10
Fax: 01 44 59 25 15
Email: ial@calva.net
Web: http://www.lorriman.demon.co.uk/ial/ialhome.htm

Hours/wk: 30
Price/wk (FF): 3300
Class size: 5-10
Min. stay: 1 week
Min. age: 16
Open: All year

Exams: CCIP

Special courses: French for business

Other useful points: The Institute is the official training centre of the Franco-British Chamber of Commerce. It is located in the Marais, near the Bastille. Students are encouraged to discover the area via their teacher.

INSTITUT PARISIEN
de langue et de civilisation françaises

Learning French in Paris

Intensive Courses:

❑ **courses start every week** for the duration of your choice (10, 15 or 25 hours per week)

❑ **12 students** maximum per class

❑ **8 levels** of general language all year round

❑ **qualified teachers** guided by two directors of studies

❑ free placement test and **personalized information in 5 languages**

❑ **no class cancellation guarantee** even in case of teacher absence or class of low attendance.

Special «au pair» program:

❑ **program with 4½ hours per week** (October through June) : general or specialized language (literature, tourism and hotel industry, Business French). *Preparation for the diplomas of the Institut Parisien, the Paris Chamber of Commerce and the Sorbonne.*

French Civilisation:

❑ <u>**FREE OF CHARGE**</u> *(for the students of the Institut Parisien)* **lectures of 1½ hours per week about French civilisation** (literature, art history, painting...)

❑ **courses on French culinary arts and/or French fashion** : 3 hours per week (all year round)

❑ **cultural activities:** twice a month

❑ **French cinema:** presentation, screening and debate

❑ **housing service:** host families selected with care, two or three-star-hotels, student hostels, airport transfer.

Sample fees (1999) : course of 15 hours per week, from 930 FF per week

OPEN ALL YEAR ROUND

Institut Parisien 87, boulevard de Grenelle. 75015 PARIS
Tel: 01.40.56.09.53   Fax: 01.43.06.46.30
Email: institut.parisien@dial.oleane.com

International House - Chantilly
European Bible Institute, Château de Lamorlaye, 60260 Lamorlaye.
administrative address:
20 Passage Dauphine, 75006 Paris
Tel: 01 44 41 80 20 Fax: 01 44 41 80 21
Email: 106310.1071@compuserve.com
Web: http://www.ilcgroup.com/french/chantilly.html

Hours/wk: 15
Price/wk (FF): from 2750
Class size: 15 max.
Min. stay: 2 weeks
Min. age: 12-17
Open: June-August

Accommodation: Full-board accommodation with families or residence included in the price.

Other useful points: Centre is located in 6 hectares of grounds, in a 120 year old château. Sports include football, badminton and volleyball. Activities and excursions at no extra cost. Beginners and advanced levels NOT accepted.

International Language Centres
Group: International House - Paris
20 Passage Dauphine
75006 Paris
Tel: 01 44 41 80 20
Fax: 01 44 41 80 21
Email: 106310.1071@compuserve.com
Web: http://www.ilcgroup.com/french/

Hours/wk: 15
Price/wk (FF): from 3250/wk
Min. stay: 2 weeks
Min. age: 16-20 (see below)
Open: July & August

Accommodation:
Half-board accommodation with families or in residence included in the price.

Other useful points:
In addition to the junior summer programmes, the centre offers 1-1 tuition for adults and closed groups throughout the year.

Language Studies International
350 rue St Honoré
75001 Paris
Tel: 01 42 60 53 70
Fax: 01 42 61 41 36
Email: par@lsi.edu
Web: http://www.lsi.edu

Hours/wk: 17-25
Price/wk (FF): 1825-2288
Min. stay: 1 week
Min. age: 16
Open: All year

Exams: DELF, CCIP

Accommodation: Families

Special courses: French for commerce / economics, business and secretaries

Other useful points: Range of courses offered with part group and part 1-1 tuition. Guided visits and day trips.

Languages Plus
Rue Rougemont
75009 Paris
Worldwide enrolment:
Tel: Canada: ++1 416 925 7117
Fax: Canada: ++1 416 925 5990
Email: info@LanguagesPlus.com
Web: http://www.LanguagesPlus.com

Hours/wk: 20-30
Price/wk (FF): On application
Class size: 20-30
Min. stay: 1 week
Min. age: 18
Open: All year

Exams: DELF / DALF

Accommodation: Families or foyers.

Other useful points: Full programme of cultural activities.

Langue Onze
15 rue Gambey
75011 Paris
Tel: 01 43 38 22 87
Fax: 01 43 38 36 01
Email: langue11@club-internet.fr
Web: http://www.langue-onze.com

Hours/wk: 4-20
Price/wk (FF): 200-825
Class size: 3-9
Min. stay: 2 weeks
Min. age: 18
Open: All year

Accommodation: Families

Other useful points: Language exchanges with French speakers. Cinema evening.

Linguarama
6 rue de Berri
75008 Paris
Tel: 01 40 76 07 07
Fax: 01 40 76 07 74
Email: caroledistilli@linguarama.com
Web: http://www.linguarama.com

Hours/wk: 20-40
Price/wk (FF): 10,000 + tax
Class size: 1-1 or 6 max.
Min. stay: 1½ hours
Min. age: 17
Open: All year

Accommodation: Families, studios, apartments or hotels.

Special courses: French for business

L'Etoile
38 Blvd Raspail
75007 Paris
Tel: 01 45 48 00 05
Fax: 01 45 48 62 05

Hours/wk: 10-20
Price (FF): 5700/ term (during year)
3500/mth (July)
Class size: 5-20
Min. stay: 1 mth (summer)
Min. age: 16
Open: All year (except Aug)

Accommodation: Families or foyers

Other useful points: Wine & cheese tasting. Social evenings arranged by the teachers.

Linguarama
Tour Eve
La Defense 9
92806 Paris La Defense
Tel: 01 47 73 13 05
Fax: 01 47 73 86 04
Email: defense@linguarama.com
Web: http://www.linguarama.com

Hours/wk: 1½-42½
Price (FF): 390 per hour
Class size: 1-1 courses
Min. stay: 1 week
Min. age: 18
Open: All year

Accommodation: Families, studios, apartments or hotels.

Special courses: French for business.

Other useful points: Resource centre.

Lutèce Langues
31, rue Etienne Marcel
75001 Paris
Tel: 01 42 36 31 51
Fax: 01 42 36 31 51
Email: lutecela@club-internet.fr

Hours/wk: 3-15
Price/wk (FF): 270-1140
Class size: 2-6
Min. stay: 1 week
Min. age: None
Open: All year

Accommodation: Families, foyers, residences, studio, apartments or hotels.

Special courses: French for business. Cookery, wine and literature courses.

Paris Langues
30 rue Cabanis
75014 Paris
Tel: 01 45 65 05 28
Fax: 01 45 81 26 28
Email: parislangues@compuserve.com

Hours/wk: 10-25 (see below)
Price/wk (FF): 825-1170 (see below)
Class size: 4-12
Min. stay: 2 weeks
Min. age: 16
Open: All year

Exams: DELF / DALF, CCIP

Accommodation: Families, residences or hotels

Special courses: Available on request

Other useful points: Special au-pair courses: 6/hrs per wk = 2600FF / term. 1-1 tuition and learning at your teacher's home also offered.

Metropolitan Languages
151, rue de Billancourt
92100 Boulogne
Tel: 01 46 04 57 32
Fax: 01 46 04 57 12
Email: metlang@calva.net

Hours/wk: depends on level
Price (FF): 400FF/hr (1-1 tuition)
Class size: 1-1 or max 6 if groups
Min. stay: None
Min. age: 18
Open: All year

Special courses: French for business. Presentation techniques.

Other useful points: Courses for company employees only. Evening excursions possible (theatre, cinema etc.)

PERL (Paris Ecole des Roches Langues)
6/ 8 rue Spinoza
75011 Paris
Tel: 01 47 00 99 98
Fax: 01 43 57 14 46
Email: cmk.roch@infonie.fr
Web: http://www.ecoledesRoches.com

Hours/wk: 3-26
Price/wk (FF): 213-1430 (approx.)
Class size: 5-15
Min. stay: 2 weeks
Min. age: 17
Open: All year

Exams: DELF / DALF, CCIP

Accommodation: Families, residences and hotels

Special courses: French for business, commerce/economics

Other useful points: Language laboratory, conferences, book loans and excursions.

Regent International
82, rue Lauriston
75116 Paris
Tel: 01 44 05 04 09
Fax: 01 44 05 04 15
Email: regent@club-internet.fr

Hours/wk: 10-25
Price/wk (FF): 5000-12,500
Class size: 10 max.
Min. age: 18
Open: All year

Accommodation: The centre does not provide open enrolment classes. Pre-arranged classes only. Contact them for further details.

Special courses: French for law, banking and tourism.

Université de la Sorbonne Nouvelle-Paris III
19, rue des Bernardins, 75005 Paris
Tel: 01 44 32 05 75
Fax: 01 43 32 05 73

Hours/wk: 10-30
Price (FF): 3400/semester, 3100/ for 20 days during summer
Class size: 20
Min. stay: 20 days (summer)
Min. age: 18
Open: Nov-Feb, Feb-June, July, Sept

Accommodation: List of addresses supplied to students

Special courses: Courses for teachers

Other useful points: Phonetics courses with lots of language laboratory tuition. Not for complete beginners. The 2nd semester, from Feb-June, is aimed at FLE teachers. Further study at the university (degrees, masters etc) is possible.

SILC Accueil France
Hôtel de la Faye
5, Rue Ste Croix de la Bretonnerie
75004 Paris
Tel: 01 48 87 60 14
Fax: 01 48 87 59 96
Email: silc.accueil@silc.fr
Web: http://www.silc.org

Hours/wk: 18-27 (approx.)
Price (FF): from 2600/2wks
Class size: 12 max.
Min. stay: 2 weeks
Min. age: 18
Open: All year

Accommodation: Families or residences.

Other useful points: Air-conditioned classrooms and a medieval garden! SILC also arranges work experience courses, 1-1 tuition and homestay programmes (living & learning with your teacher).

2 NORTHERN FRANCE

This area, not always well known to tourists, offers many interesting sights.

The southern part of the Flanders plain has a rich display of ancient castles, hidden away in beautiful forests.

Lille is the major city of this region. Only 15 kilometres from the Belgian border, it has retained a strong Flemish flavour. The birth place of General de Gaulle, it boasts excellent museums, an eclectic range of architecture and an efficient, high-tech underground system. After browsing through the largest bookshop in the world, you might like to enjoy a cool beer, for in this region of France lager is more popular than wine.

Amiens, a smaller town, is well known for its beautiful cathedrals with many spires climbing high over the city. Jules Verne wrote some of his most famous works here, and it is possible to see a display about his life at the *Centre de Documentation Jules Verne.*

Boulogne-sur-mer is a busy fishing port, perhaps best known as a destination for day-trippers from England. It has a very French atmosphere, with many cafés and restaurants, and is the most attractive of the channel ports.

AVERAGE TEMPERATURES FOR THE NORTH (° C):

Jan / Mar	Apr / Jun	Jul / Sep	Oct / Dec
6.5 / 8	14 / 21.5	23 / 19	15 / 7

LOW COST ACCOMMODATION:

Auberge de Jeunesse - Place Rouget de Lisle,
62200 Boulogne Sur Mer
68 FF per night (with breakfast)
TEL: (03) 21 80 14 50 FAX: (03) 21 80 45 62

Auberge de Jeunesse - Centre de Formation des Cadres
Sportifs, rue du Général Leclerc, 60100 Creil
49 FF per night (bed only)
TEL: (03) 44 25 37 66 FAX: (03) 44 24 24 45

Auberge de Jeunesse -
Place Paul Asseman, 59140 Dunkerque
46 FF per night (bed only)
TEL: (03) 28 63 36 34 FAX: (03) 28 63 24 54

Auberge de Jeunesse - 12, rue Malpart, 59000 Lille
68 FF per night (with breakfast)
TEL: (03) 20 57 08 94 FAX: (03) 20 63 98 93

 DIRECTORY OF COURSES IN THIS REGION

Centre de Pratique de Langues Etrangères (CPLE)
58 rue de l'Hôpital-Militaire
59800 Lille
Tel: 03 20 63 08 44
Fax: 03 20 63 08 49
Email: cple@nordnet.fr

Hours/wk: 2-30
Price/wk (FF): Variable
Class size: 1-12
Min. stay: 1 week
Min. age: 18
Open: All year

Exams: CCIP

Accommodation: Families

Special courses: Available as 1-1 tuition

Other useful points: Resource centre and multimedia facilities.

CLARIFE - Université Catholique de Lille
27, rue d'Armentières, 59000 Lille
Tel: 03 20 57 92 19 Fax: 03 20 15 29 30
Email: 101625.3230@compuserve.com

Hours/wk: 10-25
Price (FF): 4150 (9 wks), 3450 (July)
Class size: 6-25
Min. stay: 2 wks (teachers' courses), 3 wks (summer), 1 semester (year)
Min. age: 17/18
Open: All year (except Aug)

Exams: DELF / DALF, CCIP

Accommodation: Families, residences, foyers or hotels.

Special courses: European studies and university preparation courses.

Other useful points: Conferences & company visits. Language laboratory. Wine tasting and social evenings organised.

Demos Langues
15, rue de Bourgogne
59800 Lille
Tel: 03 20 30 76 80
Fax: 03 20 78 28 95
Email: langues@demos.fr
Web: http://www.demos.fr

Hours/wk: ½-40
Price/wk (FF): On application
Class size: 1-6
Min. stay: 10 hours
Min. age: 11
Open: All year

Special courses: French for business. Business life in France.

Other useful points: Part of 'Groupe Demos' which has over 25 years experience in business training.

Université Charles de Gaulle Lille III
Département des Etudiants Etrangers
BP 149, 59653 Villeneuve-d'Ascq Cdx
Tel: 03 20 41 62 96 Fax: 03 20 47 23 62
Email: dee@univ-lille3.fr
Web: http://www.uinv-lille3.fr

Hours/wk: 15-18
Price (FF): 3400 (semester), 5700 (yr)
Class size: 15-25
Min. stay: 1 semester (2 wks teachers' courses)
Min. age: 18 (with equivalent of baccalaureate)
Open: Oct-June

Exams: DELF/DALF, CPLF, DEF, DSEF

Accommodation: Families, residences or foyers.

Special courses: 19th century literature, French for business or economics. Courses for teachers.

Other useful points: Excursions, guided visits and social evenings arranged.

Université d'été de Boulogne/ Mer
BP 149
59653 Villeneuve-d'Ascq Cedex
Tel: 03 20 91 97 66
Fax: 03 20 47 23 25
Email: gamblin@univ-lille3.fr

Hours/wk: 20-25
Price (FF): 2800 (3 wks)
Class size: 15-18
Min. stay: 2-3 weeks
Min. age: 17
Open: July & August

Exams: DELF / DALF

Accommodation: Families or university residence.

Special courses: French for business, French & tennis, French & cookery. Courses for teachers.

Other useful points: Language laboratory and computers. Conversation classes in afternoon. Wide range of activities and excursions.

3 EASTERN FRANCE

The Alsace region has retained a strong Germanic flavour. Its traditional half-timbered houses topped by storks' nests and its local dialect make this region very different from any other in France.

Strasbourg, its capital, offers a contrast of old and new. A pink cathedral, cobbled streets and 19th century mansions cohabit happily with the modern hotels and conference centres built for Strasbourg's new role in Europe.

The Lorraine region is famous for its prestigious crystal industry (St. Louis, Baccarat, Daum, Sèvres etc.) and those looking for bargains will find factory outlet shops offering discounts of up to 40%.

Nancy, Lorraine's capital, is a city full of delight and surprises. Its sumptuous Place Stanislas, old town, fountains and iron gates are but a few of the many attractions of this lively and friendly city. The birth place of Art Nouveau, Nancy remains firmly a European cultural centre with a very large student population.

The Champagne region owes its reputation to its sparkling wines. Champagne cellars are always a great attraction, the best 'tasting routes' being from Epernay to Reims and the area east of Troyes.

Reims is well known for its magnificent gothic cathedral, enlightened by two beautiful rose windows. It also has the largest Romanesque church in France: the Basilique Saint Rémi, not to mention museums such as the Palais du Tau and the Salle de Reddition (General Eisenhower's room in the second world war).

The Burgundy region is famous for its vineyards. It is a lovely area of France and a good way to enjoy its beauty is to hire a boat and cruise along its 1200 kilometres of canals and rivers.

Dijon, home of the popular mustard, is one of the most enchanting towns in France. Romantic, graceful buildings from the Middle Ages and Renaissance are a joy to be seen. A large student population adds vivacity and zest to this charming old town.

AVERAGE TEMPERATURES FOR THE EAST (° C):

Jan / Mar	Apr / Jun	Jul / Sep	Oct / Dec
5.5 / 9.5	14.5 / 23	24 / 21	15 / 5

 LOW COST ACCOMMODATION:

Auberge de Jeunesse - 'Les Oiseaux', 48, rue des Cras, Les Oiseaux, 25000 Besançon
68 FF per night (with breakfast)
TEL: (03) 81 88 43 11 FAX: (03) 81 80 77 97

Auberge de Jeunesse - 1, rue de Carcassonne, 52000 Chaumont Cedex
49 FF per night (bed only)
TEL: (03) 25 03 22 77

Auberge de Jeunesse - 1, bd Champollion, 21000 Dijon
68 FF (with breakfast)
TEL: (03) 80 72 95 20 FAX: (03) 80 70 00 61

Auberge de Jeunesse - Parc Léo Lagrange, Allée Polonceau, 51100 Reims
49 FF (bed only)
TEL: (03) 26 40 52 60 FAX: (03) 26 47 35 70

Auberge de Jeunesse - rue des Cavaliers, BP 58, 67017 Strasbourg Cedex
68 FF per night (with breakfast)
TEL: (03) 88 45 54 20 FAX: (03) 88 45 54 21

A ➤ Z　DIRECTORY OF COURSES IN THIS REGION

Afpi Aisne - Centre d'Etudes des Langues
rue Jean Papillon
02100 Saint Saint-Dizier
Tel: 03 23 06 07 40
Fax: 03 23 06 07 49
Email: Informatique@Europost.com

Group courses, 1-1 tuition and in-company training.

Prepares students for the Certificat Européen (ICC).

Specialist courses available on request.

Association Internationale Langues et Cultures
1a place des Orphelins
67000 Strasbourg
Tel: 03 88 24 18 92
Fax: 03 88 37 97 25

Hours/wk: 3-4 (15+ workshops during summer)
Price (FF): 2700/3mths during year, 3555/mth summer (approx.)
Class size: 3-8
Min. stay: 3 mths (1 mth summer)
Min. age: 18
Open: All year

Accommodation: Families, foyers or residences

Special courses: French for business. Courses for teachers.

Other useful points: Library and video access.Organised visits and excursions.

Alliance Française de Bourgogne
29, rue Sambin
21000 Dijon
Tel: 03 80 72 59 92
Fax: 03 80 72 59 92

Hours/wk: 2½-20
Price (FF): 50 / hour
Class size: Variable
Min. age: 16
Open: All year

Exams: CCIP and Alliance Française

Accommodation: Families or foyers

Special courses: French for tourism and hotels.

Other useful points: Wine tasting trips and various guided visits.

C.A.FO.L- Ecole des Mines
Parc de Saurupt
BP 3106
54042 Nancy cedex
Tel: 03 83 58 42 32
Fax: 03 83 57 97 94

Hours/wk: 4-24
Price/wk (FF): 300-960
Class size: 8-16
Min. stay: 1 week
Min. age: All ages
Open: All year (except Christmas)

Exams: DELF / DALF

Accommodation: Residences or hotels

Special courses: Available as 1-1 tuition (350FF/hr)

Other useful points: Guided visits, weekend trips to Paris and range of other excursions offered.

CCI - CEL Epinal
10 rue Claude-Gelée
88026 Epinal cdx
Tel: 03 29 35 18 14
Fax: 03 29 64 01 88

1-1 tuition (330FF per hour) or in-company training.

CIEL de Strasbourg
Le Concorde
4 quai Kléber
67000 Strasbourg
Tel: 03 88 22 02 13
Fax: 03 88 75 73 70
Email: ciel.francais@strasbourg.cci.fr

Hours/wk: 15-30
Price/wk (FF): 871-1122
Class size: 10 (yr) / 15 (summer)
Min. stay: 2 weeks
Min. age: 18
Open: Jan-Dec

Exams: CCIP, Alliance Française

Accommodation: Families, foyer, residence, studios or hotels.

Special courses: French for business or tourism. Courses for teachers. Tailor-made courses for universities or companies.

Other useful points: Courses start every fortnight. Reduced rates for longer stays.

Centre de Linquistique Appliquée (Université de Franche-Comté)
6, rue Gabriel Plançon
25030 Besançon Cedex
Tel: 03 81 66 52 00 Fax: 03 81 66 52 25
Email: cla@univ.fcomte.fr
Web: http://www.univ-fcomte.fr/cla/cla.html

Hours/wk: 25-30 (intensive courses)
Price/wk (FF): 1025 (5400 semester)
Class size: 15-18
Min. stay: 2 weeks
Min. age: 16
Open: All year

Exams: DELF/DALF, CPLF, DEF, DSEF

Accommodation: Families, residences, studios or hotels.

Special courses: French for business, science & technology, tourism. Courses for teachers.

Other useful points: 1-1 tuition also available. Facilities include a language laboratory, reading room, self-service video and audio centre. Organised activities throughout the year.

CILS - Centre International Linguistique et Sportif
1 route de Paris
51700 Troissy
Tel: 03 26 52 73 08
Fax: 03 26 52 72 07
Email: CILS.FLE@wanadoo.fr
Web: http://www.dsoft.fr/cils

Hours/wk: 15
Price/wk (FF): 3775
Class size: 8-12
Min. stay: 2 weeks
Min. age: 7-18
Open: 13th June-4th Sept

Accommodation: At the centre - included in the price

Other useful points: Students can choose from 26 sports each day and there are also organised excursion. The centre has a library & computer room.

La Cardère - Institut Culturel de Langue Française
71580 Frontenaud
Tel: 03 85 74 83 11
Fax: 03 85 74 82 25
Email: la.cardere@wanadoo.fr

Hours/wk: 15hrs theory + 45 hrs conversation
Price/wk (FF): 4100-5500
Class size: 1-8
Min. stay: 1-4 weeks
Min. age: 12
Open: Feb-Dec

Accommodation: Accommodation at the Institut is included in the price (half board).

Special courses: French for business introduction.

Other useful points: Teachers present from 8am to 8pm and French is spoken all day, even at meal times. There are also 4 accompanied excursions each week.

Linguarama Dijon
Amphypolis, 10 rue Paul Verlaine
Rond Point de l'Europe
21000 Dijon
Tel: 03 80 78 77 30
Fax: 03 80 78 77 35
Email: dijon@linguarama.com
Web: http://www.linguarama.com

Hours/wk: 22½-42½
Price/wk (FF): On application
Class size: mainly 1-1 tuition
Min. stay: flexible
Open: All year

Accommodation: Families

Special courses: Arranged according to your requirements

Other useful points: All levels from beginners to advanced. Generally aimed at intensive executive courses. Lessons can start any day of the week, but you have to let the centre know 1wk before you arrive.

Linguissimo
76 rue Plaine-des-Bouchers
67100 Strasbourg
Tel: 03 88 39 66 67
Fax: 03 88 39 62 00
Email: Bradley.stock@linguissimo.com

Hours/wk: On application
Price/wk (FF): 8820 + tax
Class size: 1-5
Min. stay: 30 hours
Min. age: 18
Open: All year

Exams: DELF

Accommodation: Families or hotels.

Special courses: Commercial correspondence, making a commercial presentation, telephone techniques

Other useful points: Multimedia facilities.

Séjour linguistique et culturel en Bourgogne
Rue du Général Leclerc
21320 Pouilly-en-Auxois
Tel: 03 80 90 60 74
Fax: 03 80 90 75 46
Email: S.L.C.B.@wanadoo.fr

Hours/wk: 3
Price/wk (FF): 1830
Class size: 8
Min. stay: 19 days
Min. age: 12-17
Open: July and August

Accommodation: Accommodation is included in the price.

Other useful points: Range of sports and cultural activities available.

Université de Nancy II - Cours d'Eté pour Etudiants Etrangers
23 boulevard Albert 1er
54015 Nancy Cedex
Tel: 03 83 96 43 92
Fax: 03 83 30 64 09
Email: taveneau@clsh.u-nancy.fr

Hours/wk: 21-25
Price/wk (FF): 950
Class size: 10-15
Min. stay: 2 weeks
Min. age: 16
Open: July only

Accommodation: Residence

Special courses: Commercial French

Other useful points: All inclusive packages available: 2wks = 5000FF, 3 wks =6600FF, 4wks =7650FF. Range of excursions & activities.

Université de Bourgogne
Centre International d'Etudes Françaises
Esp. Erasme, BP 2821001 Dijon Cdx
Tel: 03 80 39 35 60 Fax: 03 80 39 35 61
Email: cief@u-bourgogne.fr
Web:http://www.u-bourgogne.fr/
Etranger/cief.html

Hours/wk: 16-22
Price/wk (FF): 1020-1250
Class size: 15-20
Min. stay: 2 weeks
Min. age: 18
Open: All year
Exams: DELF/DALF,CPLF,DEF,DSEF

Accommodation: Families, foyers, residence or studios.

Special courses: Intensive spoken French, courses for teachers, French for business, evening courses, made to measure programmes & cookery courses.

Other useful points: Linguistic & cultural workshops, introduction to life & history of Bourgogne, guided visits, cultural activities etc.

Université de Nancy II (SUEE)
23 boulevard Albert 1er
54000 Nancy
Tel: 03 83 96 70 05
Fax: 03 83 96 70 05
Email: orpel@clsh.u-nancy.fr
Web: http://www.nancy2.u-nancy.fr

Hours/wk: 15
Price (FF): 3475 (semester)
Class size: 20
Min. stay: 1 semester
Min. age: 18
Open: Oct to May

Exams: DELF / DALF, CPLF, DEF, DSEF

Accommodation: Residences or studios

Other useful points: 1 month courses for ERASMUS students (free of charge). Video and computer room, language centre and reading room.

Université de Reims -
Champagne-Ardenne
Centre International d'Etudes Françaises
32, rue Ledru-Rollin
51100 Reims
Tel: 03 26 47 04 11
Fax: 03 26 47 05 40

Hours/wk: 7-20
Price/wk (FF): 250-750
Class size: 3-20
Min. stay: 2 weeks
Min. age: 18
Open: 1st Sept-30th July

Exams: DELF/DALF, CPLF, DEF, DSEF

Accommodation: Families, foyers, residences or studios

Other useful points: Cultural activities, theatre workshop, excursions to Paris and Strasbourg. Library and self-service language laboratory.

Université de Sciences Humaines de
Strasbourg
Palais Universitaire, 9 Pl. de l'Université
67084 Strasbourg cedex
Tel: 03 88 35 53 22 Fax: 03 88 25 08 63
Email: ief@ushs.u-strasbg.fr
Web: http://130.79.140.19/default.html

Hours/wk: 15
Price (FF): 4300/sem, 1800/2wks summer
Class size: 12-20
Min. stay: 2 wks (summer)
Min. age: 18
Open: All year (except Aug & Sept)

Exams: DELF/DALF, CPLF, DEF, DSEF

Accommodation: University residences (summer only)

Special courses: Courses for teachers.

Other useful points: Summer courses in July only. Social events with French students arranged, as are cinema trips and excursions.

UNIVERSITÉ DE REIMS CHAMPAGNE-ARDENNE
Centre International d'Etudes Françaises

Reims, ville historique des sacres, du champagne, à quelques heures de Londres, proximité de Paris sans ses inconvénients.

❏ **Cours de juillet:** 15 h / semaine - 4 semaines - 2 900 Frs
(avec programme culturel inclus)

❏ **Cours pour professeurs:** 23 h / semaine - 2 semaines en juillet - 1 250 Frs

❏ **Cours de septembre:** 25 h / semaine - 4 semaines - 2 400 Frs

❏ **Cours semestriel:** 15 h / semaine - 14 semaines d'octobre à janvier et de février à mai - 3 500 Frs / semestre

❏ **Examens:** DELF, DALF, CPLF, DEF, DSEF

Atelier théâtre, programme culturel (forfait ou à la carte) :
excursions à Paris, Strasbourg, conférences, cours de cuisine etc..

Pour tout renseignement, s'adresser à l'adresse ci-dessous.

Université de Reims Champagne-Ardenne
Centre International d'Etudes Françaises, 32, rue Ledru Rollin, 51100 Reims.
Tél: +33 (0) 3 26 47 04 11 Fax: +33 (0) 3 26 47 05 40

4 SOUTH EAST FRANCE

Lyon, a 2000 years old city is second only to Paris. Its excellent facilities include splendid museums, a first class university, delightful old buildings and elegant shopping quarter. There is much to enjoy in Lyon, including sampling some of its gastronomic delights.

Grenoble, the major city in the French Alps, hosted the 1968 Winter Olympics and attracts students from around the world. It has a rich cultural heritage but also enjoys a very high-tech profile in the computer and micro-chip industries.

Avignon, once the capital of the Christian world, this delightful town is proud of its 14th Century Papal Palace. The town's 12th century bridge (le pont d' Avignon) has inspired what is probably France's best known folk-song, learnt in classrooms around the world. Avignon also hosts a yearly summer festival, a major showcase for European theatrical talent, which deserves its world-wide reputation.

Aix-en-Provence is a sophisticated city, filled with fountains, smart boulevards, grand squares and elegant houses. It is always packed with students and attracts lots of overseas visitors wishing to learn the language.

Montpellier, only a few kilometres away from the Mediterranean, this ancient city is home to one of France's biggest universities. A vibrant, lively city bathed in sunshine, it is an obvious choice for many students.

Perpignan has a strong Spanish flavour, with palm trees and squares paved with marble. It has a fun, friendly atmosphere and is ideally situated for exploring the Pyrenees.

Nice is a fashionable resort whose genoese style architecture dates from the Middle Ages. It is home to many first class museums, such as the Musée Matisse and the Musée Chagall. The city also makes a good base for visiting the popular Riviera resorts such as Cannes and Monaco.

AVERAGE TEMPERATURES FOR THE SOUTH EAST (° C):

Jan / Mar	Apr / Jun	Jul / Sep	Oct / Dec
12 / 13	18 / 26.5	28 / 25	21 / 14

 LOW COST ACCOMMODATION:

Auberge de Jeunesse - 3, avenue Marcel Pagnol,
Le Jas de Bouffan, 13090 Aix-en-Provence
49 FF per night (bed only)
TEL: (04) 42 20 15 99 FAX: (04) 42 59 36 12

Auberge de Jeunesse (Grenoble) - 10, avenue
du Grésivaudan, 'La Quinzaine', 38130 Echirolles
49 FF per night (bed only)
TEL: (04) 76 09 33 52 FAX: (04) 76 09 38 99

Auberge de Jeunesse Internationale (Lyon) -
51, rue Roger Salengro, 69200 Venissieux
49 FF per night (bed only)
TEL: (04) 78 76 39 23 FAX: (04) 78 77 51 11

Auberge de Jeunesse -
Impasse du Dr. Bonfils, 13008 Marseille
49 FF per night (bed only)
TEL: (04) 91 73 21 81 FAX: (04) 91 73 97 23

Auberge de Jeunesse - rue des Ecoles Laïques
(Impasse Petite Corraterie), 34000 Montpellier
46 FF per night (bed only)
TEL: (04) 67 60 32 22 FAX: (04) 67 60 32 30

Auberge de Jeunesse -
route forestière du Mont-Alban, 06300 Nice
46 FF per night (bed only)
TEL: (04) 93 89 23 64 FAX: (04) 92 04 03 10

Auberge de Jeunesse - Parc de la Pépinière,
avenue de Grande Bretagne, 66000 Perpignan
46 FF per night (bed only)
TEL: (04) 68 34 63 32 FAX: (04) 68 51 16 02

A ➡ Z DIRECTORY OF COURSES IN THIS REGION

ABM
6 rue des Loriots - BP 9617
34054 Montpellier cedex 01
Tel: 04 67 02 75 00
Fax: 04 67 02 76 00
Email: abm@wanadoo.fr

Hours/wk: 20-25
Price/wk (FF): from 850 (see below)
Class size: 5-12
Min. stay: 2 weeks
Min. age: 16
Open: June to August

Exams: CCIP

Accommodation: Families, residences or studios.

Special courses: French & cookery. French for business. Courses for teachers.

Other useful points: Special all inclusive packages available: tuition, full board accommodation and activities from 5800 FF for 2 wks.

Actilangue Ecole Privée de Langue Française
2 rue Alexis Mossa
06000 Nice
Tel: 04 93 96 33 84
Fax: 04 93 44 37 16
Email: actilang@imaginet.fr

Hours/wk: 20-30
Price/wk (FF): from 770
Class size: 3-12
Min. stay: 1 wk (summer)
Min. age: 16
Open: All year

Exams: CCIP

Accommodation: Families, apartments or hotels

Special courses: Commercial / business French

Other useful points: 1-1 tuition also offered. Library and self-service audio/ video rooms. Group excursions to neighbouring towns.

Alliance Française
2 rue de Paris, 06000 Nice
Tel: 04 93 62 67 66 Fax: 04 93 85 28 06
Email: af-nice@webstore.fr
Web: http://www.webstore.fr/alliance-francise-nice

Hours/wk: 4-20
Price/wk (FF): 150-725
Class size: 7-16
Min. stay: 1 week
Min. age: 18 (or 16 if parental permission given)
Open: All year

Exams: DEFL / DALF, CCIP and Alliance Française

Accommodation: Families, residences, studios or hotels.

Special courses: French for business or tourism. Courses for teachers.

Other useful points: Library and self-service multimedia centre. Guided museum and company visits. Social evenings.

Alliance Française
11, rue Pierre Bourdan, 69003 Lyon
Tel: 04 78 95 24 72
Fax: 04 78 60 77 28
Email: alliance-francaise-lyon@compuserve.com

Hours/wk: 4-20
Price/wk (FF): 600-2400 (see below)
Class size: 7-15
Min. stay: 1 month
Min. age: 16
Open: All year

Exams: DELF / DALF & Alliance Française

Accommodation: Families and university residence (summer only)

Special courses: French for business, literature, history (as optional extras)

Other useful points: Summer intensive courses - 54 hrs in 18 days = 2000 FF, 90 hrs in 18 days = 3300 FF. Various workshops offered. Optional excursions, guided visits etc.

Alliance Française
55 rue Paradis
13006 Marseille
Tel: 04 91 33 28 19
Fax: 04 91 33 70 30

Hours/wk: 6-20
Price/wk (FF): 225-675
Class size: 10-22
Min. stay: 1 week
Min. age: 16
Open: Sept-July

Exams: Alliance Française

Accommodation: Families, residences, studios, apartments or hotels.

Special courses: Various options on request

Other useful points: Only intensive courses offered in July. Range of excursions, conferences etc.

Alliance Française
6 rue Boussairolles
34000 Montpellier
Tel: 04 67 58 92 74
Fax: 04 67 92 90 83

Hours/wk: 15-20
Price (FF): 2600 (4wks)
Class size: 8-12
Min. stay: 3 weeks
Min. age: 17
Open: All year

Exams: DELF / DALF & Alliance Française

Accommodation: Families or residences

Other useful points: Literary readings by actors and various visits and excursions.

Alpha-B Institut Linquistique
7 Bd Prince de Galles, 06000 Nice
Tel: 04 93 53 11 10 Fax: 04 93 53 11 20
Email: alpha.b@webstore.fr
Web: http://www.alpha-b.fr

Hours/wk: 15-22½
Price/wk (FF): 1000-1450
Class size: 4-10
Min. stay: 2 weeks
Min. age: 16
Open: All year

Exams: DELF

Accommodation: Families, apartments or hotels.

Special courses: Available as 1-1 tuition

Other useful points: 'A'-level / baccalaureate level courses for secondary school students (Easter & summer). Self-service video-room, library and internet use. French films shown twice a week. Workshops on wine, history of art, history etc.

APRE- Institut Culturel Français
BP 5032
34032 Montpellier Cedex
Tel: 04 67 72 22 77
Fax: 04 67 79 15 28
Email: etudesfr@aol.com

Hours/wk: 25-35
Price/wk (FF): 1300
Class size: 5-8
Min. stay: 2 weeks
Min. age: 16
Open: July - August

Exams: DELF / DALF

Accommodation: Families, foyers, residences, studios, apartments or hotels.

Other useful points: Activities include excursions, trips to the seaside, theatre, restaurants, cinema etc.

Alp'lingua - Institut Alpin des Langues
352, rue des Prés, Col des Saisies
73620 Hauteluce
Tel: 04 79 38 98 80 Fax: 04 79 38 98 80
Email: AlpLingua@aol.com

Hours/wk: 12-18
Price/wk (FF): 2390-2890
Class size: 5 max
Min. stay: 1 week
Min. age: 18
Open: mid Dec - mid Sept
Exams: DELF / DALF

Accommodation: Families, studios, apartments or hotels. (Apartment and all meals included in the price).

Special courses: French for business, tourism, secretaries and teachers. Translation courses.

Other useful points: Few minutes from the ski slopes and accomodates just 10 students at a time. Various activities & sports. On site library. Yearly enrolment fee of 350 FF, + add 400 FF in the winter to cover the extra accommodation costs.

Assocation Interlangue
14 impasse de la Source
34200 Sète
Tel: 04 67 51 31 00
Fax: 04 67 43 03 82

Hours/wk: 18½
Price/wk (FF): 2300 (approx.)
Class size: 2-10
Min. stay: 2 weeks
Min. age: 17
Open: mid July to mid Aug

Exams: Certificate of Attendance only

Accommodation: Families, youth hostels or apartments

Other useful points: Activities arranged - 5 afternoons + 1 evening per stay

Association de Langue Française d'Avignon (ALFA)
4 Impasse Romagnoli, 84000 Avignon
Tel: 04 90 85 86 24 Fax: 04 90 85 89 55
Email: alfavignon@avignon.pacwan.net
Web: http://perso.pacwan.fr/alfavignon

Hours/wk: 6-30
Price/wk (FF): 1500 (15hrs) - 3500 (30hrs)
Class size: 6 max
Min. stay: 2 weeks
Min. age: 17
Open: All year

Exams: DELF / DALF, CCIP

Accommodation: Families, studios, apartments or hotels

Special courses: Courses for au-pairs, teachers + workshops (French chansons, journalism)

Other useful points: Free access video room. Excursions and themed visits arranged. Workshops on the Avignon Festival.

Azurlingua
25 Bd Raimbaldi, 06000 Nice
Tel: 04 93 62 01 11
Fax: 04 93 62 22 56
Email: Info@azurlingua.com
Web: http://www.azurlingua.com

Hours/wk: 1-35
Price/wk (FF): 720-2000
Class size: 6-10
Min. stay: 1 week
Min. age: 18
Open: Jan-Dec.

Exams: DELF / DALF, CCIP, Alliance Française

Accommodation: Families, residences, studios, apartments or hotels.

Special courses: French for business, tourism and secretaries.

Other useful points: Cultural activities and sports organised daily throughout the year. Computer room with internet access.

Audra Langues
2 bd Victor Hugo
06000 Nice
Tel: 04 93 87 23 11
Fax: 04 93 88 26 92
Email: audford@iway.fr
Web: http://www.cyberlangues.com

Hours/wk: 2-30
Price/wk (FF): On application
Class size: 6
Min. stay: 30 hours
Min. age: 15

Exams: DELF/ DALF, Alliance Française

Accommodation: Families, residences, studios, apartments or hotels.

Special courses: French for business.

BABEL
22ter, rue de France
06000 Nice
Tel: 04 93 82 27 44
Fax: 04 93 88 21 30
Email: 101755.2404@compuserve.com

Hours/wk: 15
Price/wk (FF): 1300
Class size: 4-12
Min. stay: 2 weeks
Min. age: 16-65
Open: All year

Exams: DELF / DALF (on demand for longer courses only)

Accommodation: Studios

Special courses: French for commerce and economics.

Other useful points: The school is just 100m from the beach, in the heart of Nice. The school has a language laboratory and video room.

Britannia B -
Institut d'enseignement des langues
20 , blvd Eugène-Deruelle
69432 Lyon Part-Dieu cdx 03
Tel: 04 78 62 62 60
Fax: 04 78 62 32 29

1-1 tuition from 250FF per hour.
Also private groups of 2-6
(e.g. companies etc.) from
320FF per hour

Other useful points:
Multimedia resource centre

Centre de Français Langue Etrangère
du CIHEAM
3191 route de Mende, BP 5056
34093 Montpellier cedex 5
Tel: 04 67 04 60 02 Fax: 04 67 54 25 27
Email: peral@iamm.fr
Web: http://www.iamm.fr

Hours/wk: 15-25
Price/wk (FF): 900 (20hrs/wk)
Class size: 6-12
Min. stay: 2 weeks
Min. age: 18
Open: All year

Exams: Centre's own certificates

Accommodation: Families, residences
or hotels

Special courses: French for science
(biology & agriculture)

Other useful points: Multimedia, video
and computer room. Library, language
laboratory and resource centre.
Company visits.

Campus International
BP 131, 83957 La Garde Cedex
Tel: 04 94 21 12 82 Fax: 04 94 14 30 52
Email: campus@wanadoo.fr
Web: http://perso.wanadoo.fr/
campus.international

Hours/wk: 3-21
Price/wk (FF): 200-1500
Class size: 5-15
Min. stay: 2 weeks
Min. age: 16
Open: All year

Exams: DELF / DALF, CCIP, AF

Accommodation: Families or
residences at the campus

Special courses: French for business,
Discover Provence, Methodology of
FLE

Other useful points: The centre is set
in 30 acres of grounds. Sports,
excursions and activities during the
summer. Company visits in winter.
Audio-visual room + free access
resource centre.

Centre d'Etudes Linguistiques
d'Avignon (CELA)
16 rue Sainte-Catherine, 84000 Avignon
Tel: 04 90 86 04 33 Fax: 04 90 85 92 01
Email: cela@avignon-et-provence.com
Web: http://www.avignon-et-
provence.com/cela

Hours/wk: 20-30
Price/wk (FF): 1250-2000
Class size: 3-12
Min. stay: 2 weeks
Min. age: 17
Open: All year

Exams: DELF / DALF, CCIP

Accommodation: Families, foyers,
hotels or camping.

Special courses: Business, tourism,
politics, economics, science &
technology.

Other useful points: Various
workshops (poetry, cinema etc). Sports,
cookery & excursions. Language
laboratory and video-room.

**Centre International d'Accueil
et de Formation**
Château de Deomas
BP 54, 07104 Annonay Cedex
Tel: 04 75 69 26 00 Fax: 04 75 69 26 19
Email: ciaf@mail.mairie-annonay.fr

Hours/wk: 20-30
Price/wk (FF): 1200-1800 (approx.)
Class size: 2-15
Min. stay: 1 week
Min. age: 16
Open: All year

Exams: DELF / DALF, CCIP

Accommodation: Families, residences, apartments or hotels.

Special courses: French for business, economics, science & technology. Courses for teachers.

Other useful points: The school is based in a modernised château. Facilities include a language laboratory and mediatheque. Sports and excursions arranged.

**Centre International d'Antibes/
Institut Prévert**
28, avenue du Château
06600 Antibes Cedex
Tel: 04 93 74 47 76 Fax: 04 93 74 57 11
Email: cia@imcn.com
Web: http://www.cia-France.com

Hours/wk: 20-36
Price/wk (FF): 1340-3055
Class size: 4-12
Min. stay: 2 weeks
Min. age: 18 (14 summer)
Open: All year

Exams: DELF / DALF, CCIP, Alliance Française

Accommodation: Families, residences or hotels.

Special courses: French for business, tourism and hotels. Courses for teachers.

Other useful points: Range of activities, including wine tasting and cookery classes.

Centre International des Langues
166, avenue du Majoral Arnaud
04100 Manosque
Tel: 04 92 72 46 19 Fax: 04 92 87 82 81
Email: cilangue@club-internet.fr
Web: http://www.cilang.com

Hours/wk: 16-28
Price/wk (FF): 860-3400
Class size: 1-6
Min. stay: 1 week
Min. age: 18
Open: 1st Feb-31st Nov

Exams: DELF, CCIP

Accommodation: Families, residences, studios or hotels.

Special courses: French for business. Courses for teachers. Interactive multimedia courses.

Other useful points: Multimedia language laboratories, computer facilities and mediatheque. Sightseeing trip arranged, plus wide range of sports available.

Centre Langues Sophia Antipolis
Centre International de Valbonne
rue Frédéric-Mistral, BP 097
06902 Sophia-Antipolis cdx
Tel: 04 92 96 52 50
Fax: 04 92 96 52 99
Email: civ@ac-nice.fr
Web: http://www2.ac-nice.fr/etabs/civ

Hours/wk: 15 +
Price (FF): from 5100 / 2 weeks
Min. stay: 2 weeks
Min. age: 14
Open: All year

Accommodation: Centre's own residence

Other useful points: Resource centre, with computers, CD-ROMs, audio & video facilities, library. The centre's residence also has a pool and cafeteria.

Centre Méditerranéen d'Etudes Françaises
Chemin des Oliviers, 06320 Cap d'Ail
Tel: 04 93 78 21 59 Fax: 04 93 41 83 96
Email: centremed@monte-carlo.mc
Web: http://www.monte-carlo.mc/centremed

Hours/wk: 20-30
Price/wk (FF): 1525 (30 hrs)
Class size: 5-15
Min. stay: 2 weeks
Min. age: 18 (see below)
Open: All year
Exams: CCIP & Alliance Française

Accommodation: Centre's own residence (1400/wk, half-board)

Special courses: French for business. Courses for teachers.

Other useful points: Special 'language & sports' courses for juniors (13-17 yrs) June-Aug, 6000FF / 2wks, full-board. Centre is situated in 4 hectares of grounds, with an amphitheatre designed by Jean Cocteau.

Centre Linguistique Méditerranéen
16 blvd de Stalingrad
83500 La Seyne sur Mer
Tel: 04 94 94 69 54
Fax: 04 94 87 77 39

Group lessons or 1-1 tuition.

Also courses over the telephone.

Contact the centre for more details.

College International de Cannes
1 rue du Docteur Pascal, 06400 Cannes
Tel: 04 93 47 39 29 Fax: 04 93 47 51 97
Email: cic@imaginet.fr
Web: http://user.aol.com/Cannes06/private/index.html

Hours/wk: 15-25
Price (FF): from 3500 / 4 wks
Class size: 6-15 (av. 10)
Min. stay: 2 weeks
Min. age: 18 (16 summer)
Open: All year

Exams: DELF / DALF, CCIP, Alliance Française

Accommodation: Families, on campus residence or studios.

Special courses: French for business, tourism, secretaries. Also literature, cinema & politics.

Other useful points: Work placements arranged (no salary) for students with at least an intermediate level of French. Excursions and social evenings.

Créa-langues
Le Monastère de Ségriès
04360 Moustiers-Ste-Marie
Tel: 04 92 77 74 58 Fax: 04 92 77 75 18
Email: CREA.langues@wanadoo.fr
Web: http://perso.wanadoo.fr/crea-langues

Hours/wk: See below
Price (FF): Adults: from 7100/2wks,
Children: from 4400/10 days
Class size: 5-8
Min. stay: 1 week
Min. age: 12
Open: April-Sept

Accommodation: Residential full-board accommodation is included in the price.

Special courses: French for business.

Other useful points: Adult courses (April-Sept): 3,5 or 6/7 hrs per day + activities. Children (July-Sept): 3hrs tuition/ day + activities with French children (water-sports, horse-riding etc.) The price also includes excursions.

Demos Langues
33, cours de la Liberté
69003 Lyon
Tel: 04 78 60 15 60
Fax: 04 78 62 25 18
Email: langues@demos.fr
Web: http://www.demos.fr

Hours/wk: ½-40
Price/wk (FF): On application
Class size: 1-6
Min. stay: 10 hours
Min. age: 11
Open: All year

Special courses: French for business. Business life in France.

Other useful points: Part of 'Groupe Demos' which has over 25 years experience in business training.

Demos Langues
4, place Robert Schuman
Europole
38000 Grenoble
Tel: 04 76 49 96 19
Fax: 04 76 49 94 71
Email: langues@demos.fr
Web: http://www.demos.fr

Hours/wk: ½-40
Price/wk (FF): On application
Class size: 1-6
Min. stay: 10 hours
Min. age: 11
Open: All year

Same features as the centre in Lyon.

DISCOURS & MÉTHODE
Françoise Le Roux

Specialists in one to one tuition

Intensive teaching from highly experienced professionals
Programmes individually adapted to your requirements
Luxury accommodation in central Lyon
Gastronomic cuisine
Competitive prices

See the entry on this page or visit our website via http://www.europa-pages.co.uk

The enjoyable way to learn!

Ecole de Langues Internationale - Centre Hobson
31 rue Pellisson, 34500 Béziers
Tel: 04 67 49 33 39
Fax: 04 67 28 40 63
Email: kjmac@intranet.ca
Web: http://www.centre-hobson.com

Hours/wk: 10-20
Price/wk (FF): 1125-3000
Class size: 4-8
Min. stay: 1 week
Min. age: 15
Open: All year

Exams: DELF / DALF, CCIP

Accommodation: Families, studios or hotels.

Special courses: French for business, tourism and law. Courses for teachers.

Other useful points: The centre arranges visits to local companies. Also, range of excursions, conferences and activities.

Discours et Méthode
27, Quai St Vincent, 69001 Lyon
Tel: 04 78 39 30 27
Fax: 04 78 39 30 27
Email: dismet@compuserve.com
Web: http://ourworld.compuserve.com/homepages/dismet

Hours/wk: 10-30
Price/wk (FF): 4,300
Class size: 1-1 tuition
Min. stay: None
Min. age: None
Open: All year

Accommodation: Price includes accommodation in your teacher's home, with breakfast and one gourmet meal per day.

Special courses: Courses tailor-made to the individual's requirements.

Other useful points: Access to videos, CD-ROM and other learning materials. Visits to areas of interest in the region. Specialists in 1-1 tuition.

Ecole Klesse
1 rue Victoire de la Marne
34006 Montpellier Cedex
Tel: 04 67 92 66 58 Fax: 04 67 58 17 99
Email: ecole.klesse@wanadoo.fr
Web: http://perso.wanadoo.fr/ecole.klesse

Hours/wk: 20-30
Price/wk (FF): 1675-3050
Class size: 2-6
Min. stay: 2 weeks
Min. age: 18
Open: All year

Exams: DELF / DALF & Alliance Française (an exam centre)

Accommodation: Families, residences, studios, apartments or hotels.

Special courses: French for business and tourism.

Other useful points: Mediatheque, video room and internet access. Various excursions and a cheese and wine evening.

Ecole Méditerranéenne
31, rue de l'Argenterie
34000 Montpellier
Tel: 04 67 66 14 51
Fax: 04 67 66 12 01
Email: Ecolemed@wanadoo.fr

Hours/wk: 20-26
Price/wk (FF): 1200-2600
Class size: 4-10
Min. stay: 2 wks (or 1wk if 1-1 tuition)
Min. age: 17
Open: All year

Exams: CCIP

Accommodation: Families, residences or studios

Special courses: French for business, tourism, economics & commerce, secretaries + teachers.

Other useful points: Excursions every weekend during the summer. School can also arrange courses in Martinique or Guadeloupe.

ELFCA
66, avenue de Toulon
83400 Hyères
Tel: 04 94 65 03 31
Fax: 04 94 65 81 22
Email: elfca@eflca.com
Web: http://www.elfca.com

Hours/wk: 22-30
Price/wk (FF): 1200-9600
Class size: 2-12
Min. stay: 1 week
Min. age: 16
Open: All year

Exams: Alliance Française

Accommodation: Families, studios, apartments or hotels.

Other useful points: Free access language laboratory, loan of tapes & books, organised excursions. School also has a cafeteria / restaurant and air-conditioned rooms.

EF - Nice
21 rue Meyerbeer
06000 Nice
Tel: 04 93 88 84 85
Fax: 04 93 88 10 21
Web: http://www.ef.com

Hours/wk: 20-30
Price: 1200 US$/2 wks
Class size: 12 average
Min. stay: 2 weeks

Accommodation: Full-board accommodation (families) included in the price. In July & Aug possible to stay in university residence.

Other useful points: The school has been recently refurbished. It is located just 100m from the beach. Airport transfers can be arranged (additional charge).

EUROFAEC
Association Européenne d'Education et de Culture
Montpellier-Facultés, BP 4113
34091 Montpellier Cedex 5
Tel: 04 67 68 20 15
Fax: 04 67 50 60 90
Email: eurofaec@wanadoo.fr
Web: http://perso.wanadoo.fr/eurofaec

Hours/wk: 20-23
Price/wk (FF): from 1050
Class size: 8-12
Min. stay: 2 weeks
Min. age: 16
Open: All year

Exams: DELF / DALF

Accommodation: Families or residences

Other useful points: Special intensive courses for students preparing for 'A' level / baccalaureate. All inclusive packages 5995FF / 3 weeks. Students can be met at airport or station.

Eurolingua - Espace Langues
Havre Saint Pierre
265 allée du Nouveau Monde
34000 Montpellier
Tel: 04 67 15 04 73
Fax: 04 67 15 04 73
Email: info@eurolingua.com
Web: http://www.eurolingua.com

Hours/wk: 15
Price/wk (FF): On application
Class size: 5-8 normal (12 max)
Min. stay: 1 week
Min. age: 16
Open: All year

Exams: DELF / DALF

Accommodation: Families, studios or apartments.

Other useful points: All levels from beginners to advanced. Start any Monday. Library and video room. Social evenings arranged.

Eurolingua Institute
Havre Saint Pierre
265 allée du Nouveau Monde
34000 Montpellier
Tel: 04 67 15 04 73
Fax: 04 67 15 04 73
Email: info@eurolingua.com
Web: http://www.eurolingua.com

Homestay programmes arranged throughout France.

1-1 tuition in your teacher's home, with accommodation and all meals.

For ages 16-75.

Also special theme holidays: wine tasting, cooking, skiing etc.

Fondvielle Language School
'Fondvielle' Lieu dit 'Taponas'
69620 St. Verand
Tel: 04 74 71 62 64

Hours/wk: 20
Price/wk (FF): 3000 (approx.)
Class size: 2-6
Min. stay: 1 week
Min. age: 18
Open: All year

Exams: Preparation for GCSE & 'A' level French (UK school exams).

Accommodation: Single room accommodation at the school included in the price.

Special courses: Contemporary France and French literature.

Other useful points: Wine tasting arranged. Evening of French 'chansons'

France Langue et Culture
In winter, contact: 45 B, 214 22 Malmö, Sweden Tel/Fax: 46 8350698
In summer: Le Vallis Curans B
Ave. de Valescure, 83700 St.Raphaël
Tel: 04 92 09 54 50 Fax: 04 92 09 54 50
Email: france.langue@swipnet.se
Web: http://www.algonet.se/~t-i/

Hours/wk: from 20
Price (FF): from 2900/2wks
Class size: 8-14
Min. stay: 2 weeks
Min. age: none
Open: June to Aug

Accommodation: Families, apartments or hotels.

Special courses: Business French and the European Market. Courses for teachers.

Other useful points: Activities include golf, tennis and wind-surfing. 2 wks tuition + half-board family accommodation = 4800FF

France Langue
22 avenue Notre-Dame, 06000 Nice
Tel: 04 93 13 78 88
Fax: 04 93 13 78 89
Email: frlang_n@club-internet.fr
Web: http://www.france-langue.fr

Hours/wk: 15-30
Price/wk (FF): 700-1900 (see below)
Class size: 12 max
Min. stay: 1 week
Min. age: 17
Open: All year

Exams: DELF / DALF

Accommodation: Families, residences or hotels.

Special courses: French for business, tourism and literature. Courses for teachers.

Other useful points: All inclusive youth packages offered: 3550-3900/wk with sports. Students can use the language laboratory, computers and videos at their leisure.

French Riviera Homestays
31 avenue des Baumettes, 06000 Nice
Tel: 04 93 44 12 46
Fax: 04 93 86 28 09
Email: cucchi06@hotmail.com
Web: http://www.i-france.com/
housemusic/carnavel.htm

Hours/wk: 15-25
Price/wk (FF): 4500-6400
Class size: 1-1 tuition only
Min. stay: 1-4 weeks
Min. age: 18-60
Open: All year

Exams: DELF, CCIP

Accommodation: Full board accommodation at your teacher's house is included in the price.

Special courses: French for business, French for tourism.

Other useful points: Free excursions to Monte Carlo, Cannes, St. Tropez , St Paul de Vence & local museums , using your teacher's car!'

Groupe Set
Place Sophie Laffitte
BP 127, 06903 Sophia Antipolis
Tel: 04 92 96 57 05 Fax: 04 92 96 57 01
Email: info@groupeset.com
Web: http://www.groupeset.com

Hours/wk: 10-40
Price/wk (FF): 2500
Class size: 2-8
Min. stay: 1 week
Min. age: 18
Open: All year

Exams: DELF / DALF, CCIP

Accommodation: Families, residences, studios, apartments or hotels.

Special courses: French for business. Cookery, wine and culture classes.

Other useful points: Resource centre (multimedia, films, books). Sports and excursions optional.

ILP (Institut Linguistique du Peyrou)
3 rue Auguste Comte
34000 Montpellier
Tel: 04 67 92 05 55
Fax: 04 67 92 30 10
Email: ilp@mnet.fr
Web: http://www.sspfrance.com/ilp

Hours/wk: 12-15
Price/wk (FF): 650-750
Class size: 7-12
Min. stay: 2 weeks
Min. age: 16
Open: All year

Exams: DELF / DALF

Accommodation: Families, residences, studio or hotels.

Special courses: French for business, French for tourism. Courses for teachers.

Other useful points: Library, video room, CD-ROM, language laboratory and workshops.

IDIOM
4 Bd de Cimiez
Le Majestic
06000 Nice
Tel: 04 93 92 60 90
Fax: 04 93 92 58 33

Hours/wk: 20-30
Price/wk (FF): from 2130
Class size: 3-8
Min. stay: 1 week
Min. age: 18
Open: All year

Exams: DELF

Accommodation: Families, apartments or hotels.

Special courses: French for business. Courses for teachers.

Other useful points: 1-1 tuition also offered. Also special courses for senior citizens.

ILTC
28 rue Louis Guérin
69628 Villeurbanne Cdx
Tel: 04 78 93 03 91
Fax: 04 78 93 54 89

Hours/wk: Tailor-made
Price/wk (FF): On demand
Class size: 1-1 tuition
Min. stay: 20 hours
Min. age: 18
Open: All year

Accommodation: Families or hotels

Special courses: French for business

Other useful points: Teaching method is targeted to the individual needs of the professional.

IMEF -
Espace Universitaire Albert Camus
21 avenue du Professeur Grasset
34093 Montpellier Cedex 5
Tel: 04 67 91 70 00 Fax: 04 67 91 70 01
Email: imef@fle.fr
Web: http://www.fle.fr/imef

Hours/wk: 15-21
Price/wk (FF): 1350-2400
Min. stay: 2 weeks
Min. age: 17
Open: All year

Exams: DELF / DALF

Accommodation: Families or residences.

Special courses: French for journalism/media, science, law, interpretation/translation. Courses for teachers.

Other useful points: Daily programme of activities, including conferences, excursions and sports.

Inlingua Aix en Provence
Hémiris Bât. 1, Z.I "Les Milles"
115, rue Claude Nicolas Le Doux
13854 Aix- en- Provence cdx 3
Tel: 04 92 39 49 46
Fax: 04 92 97 64 38
Email: inlinguaprovence@dial.oleane.com

Part of the international chain of Inlingua schools.

Contact the centre directly for full details.

INSA-LYON - Service de français langue étrangère
20, avenue Albert Einstein
69621 Villeurbanne Cedex
Tel: 04 72 43 83 66 Fax: 04 72 43 88 95
Email: servfran@insa-lyon.fr
Web: http://www.insa-lyon.fr/ServiceDeFrancais

Hours/wk: 25
Price/wk (FF): 980
Class size: 12 max
Min. stay: 4 weeks
Min. age: 18
Open: All year (except July)

Exams: DELF / DALF

Accommodation: Families, residences, studios or hotels.

Special courses: French for science & technology. Business & management. Economics & commerce.

Other useful points: Restaurant, multimedia centre, library and video room. Events and conferences arranged all year.

INSTED - Institute of Foreign Education
BP 131
74 404 Chamonix Mont-Blanc
Tel: 05 46 41 21 39
Email: info@insted.se
Web: http://www.insted.se

Hours/wk: 20
Price (FF): 12,800/16 wks
Class size: 20 average
Min. stay: 16 wks
Min. age: 18
Open: Jan-May (with Easter break)

Exams: DELF / DALF

Accommodation: Shared apartments with other students

Other useful points: All levels from beginners to advanced. Courses are run in co-operation with Université de Stendhal-Grenoble III.

Institut de Français
23 ave Général Leclerc,
06230 Villefranche-sur-Mer
Tel: 04 93 01 88 44
Fax: 04 93 76 92 17
Email: instfran@aol.com
Web: http://www.institutdefrancais.com

Hours/wk: 40
Price (FF): 14,700-16,700 / 4 wks
Class size: 10
Min. stay: 2 weeks
Min. age: 21
Open: All year

Accommodation: Families, studios or apartments.

Special courses: Introduction to French for business (advanced levels only)

Other useful points: The Institut arranges day-trips, outings to the cinema & restaurant etc.

Institut Français d'Annecy (IFALPES)
Les Marquisats
52 rue des Marquisats
74000 Annecy
Tel: 04 50 45 38 37
Fax: 04 50 45 86 72
Email: infos@ifalpes.fr
Web: http://www.ifalpes.fr

Hours/wk: 20-30
Price/wk (FF): 430-715
Class size: 12-18
Min. stay: 2 weeks
Min. age: 16
Open: All year

Exams: DELF / DALF, CCIP, CPLF, DEF

Accommodation: Families, foyers, residence, studios or hotels

Special courses: French for business, teacher refresher courses, DELF / DALF preparation courses.

Other useful points: Organised cultural activities, sports and entertainment.

INSTITUT FRANÇAIS D'ANNECY

Annecy is in the South East of France, situated on the lake of the same name, at an altitude of 450m (1350ft). Greater Annecy has 100 000 inhabitants and its proximity to the beaches and National parks in summer, and the ski resorts in winter, provides the students with cultural and athletic activities within a pleasant urban environment. The institute is located near the medieval town centre, close to the lake.

The French Institute of Annecy is a leading French language training centre, operating with the co-operation and approval of institutes both in France & abroad. We welcome students from all over the world and of all ages. We are open all year round and our capacity is controlled in order to ensure high standards. Diplomas from the Catholic University of Lyon are awarded to students at the end of each session and the DELF & DALF are also prepared at Ifalpes.

Ifalpes has its own accommodation service which guarantees the choice of a place in a shared apartment, studio, student residence or French family (half-board).

Numerous cultural & leisure activities are organised by Ifalpes including visits to: Chamonix -Mont Blanc, The Chartreuse, Geneva, Cannes, Grenoble, Lyon and the Beaujolais region. As well as tennis, football, sailing, hikes, aerobics, horse-riding and weekly ski trips to the biggest ski resorts in the Alps.

Centre de résidence des Marquisats, 52 rue des Marquisats, 74000 ANNECY. France
Tel: (33) 04 50 45 38 37   Fax: (33) 04 50 45 86 72   E-Mail: infos@ifalpes.fr   Web: http://www.ifalpes.fr

INSTITUT FRANÇAIS DE CHAMBÉRY

Chambéry is in the South East of France, in the Alps, at an altitude of 270m (800ft) and is near to Geneva, Lyon and the Olympic ski resorts. It is a city of art and history as well as the historical capital of Savoie with 100 000 inhabitants. The Alps, Savoie & Chambéry are characterised by old castles, lakes, National parks, vineyards and summer & winter mountain activities.

Regarded as a leading French language centre, Ifalpes operates with the co-operation and approval of universities and institutes in France and abroad. We welcome students from all over the world and of all ages. We are open all year round and our capacity is controlled to ensure high standards. Diplomas from the Catholic University of Lyon are awarded to students at the end of each session and the DELF & DALF are also prepared at Ifalpes.

Ifalpes has its own accommodation service which guarantees the choice of a place in a shared apartment, studio, student residence or French family (half-board).

Many cultural and leisure activities are organised by Ifalpes including visits to: Chamonix, Mont-Blanc, The Chartreuse, Turin, Venise, Milan, Geneva, Cannes, Grenoble, Lyon & the Beaujolais region and of course, popular tourist sites in Savoie. As well as tennis, football, sailing, hikes, aerobics, horse-riding and weekly ski trips to the biggest ski resorts in the Alps.

Château de Boigne, Parc de Buisson Rond, 73000 CHAMBÉRY. France.
Tel: (33) 04 79 85 83 16 Fax: (33) 04 79 85 13 56   E-Mail: info@ifalpes.fr Web: http://www.ifalpes.fr

Institut Français de Chambéry (IFALPES)
Château de Boigne
Parc de Buisson Rond
73000 Chambéry
Tel: 04 79 85 83 16
Fax: 04 79 85 13 56
Email: info@ifalpes.fr
Web: http://www.ifalpes.fr

Hours/wk: 8-26
Price/wk (FF): 330-590
Class size: 12-18
Min. stay: 1 week
Min. age: 16
Open: All year

Exams: DELF/ DALF, CCIP, CPLF, DEF

Accommodation: Families, foyers, residences, studios or hotels

Special courses: French for business & DELF preparation classes

Other useful points: Organised cultural activities, sports and entertainment.

Institut IDEFLEN
11, rue Rostan, 06600 Antibes
Tel: 04 93 67 65 97
Fax: 04 93 67 75 71
Email: aideflen@infonie.fr
Web: http://www.infonie.fr/public-html/ideflen

Hours/wk: 15
Price/wk (FF): 950-1550
Class size: 5-15
Min. stay: 2 weeks
Min. age: 18
Open: July & August (see below)

Exams: DELF

Accommodation: Families or residence.

Special courses: French for business. Courses for teachers.

Other useful points: During the year, IDEFLEN runs courses of 20 hrs / wk, with full board accommodation - price: 4000/wk. Range of activities, minibus to beach and weekly excursions.

Institut Linguistique Adenet (ILA)
33, Grand Rue Jean Moulin
34000 Montpellier
Tel: 04 67 60 67 83 Fax: 04 67 60 67 81
Email: ILA.France@mnet.fr
Web: http://www.ila-france.com

Hours/wk: 20-30
Price/wk (FF): 1400-1950
Class size: 2-8
Min. stay: 1 week
Min. age: 16
Open: All year

Exams: DELF / DALF

Accommodation: Families, residences, studios, apartments or hotels.

Special courses: Business French, French + cooking lessons

Other useful points: 18th Century building in the heart of the city's historic centre. 3 free workshops per week (e.g. wine course, French culture). All levels from beginners to advanced. Organised excursions and activities.

Institut Lyonnais pour la Diffusion de la Langue et de la Culture Françaises
40, rue de Gerland
69007 Lyon
Tel: 04 78 69 25 04
Fax: 04 78 69 14 30
Email: ildif@asi.fr

Hours/wk: 20
Price (FF): 2800-4000 / mth
Class size: 15 max
Min. stay: 1 month
Min. age: 18
Open: All year

Accommodation: Families or residences.

Special courses: French for business or law. Courses for teachers.

Other useful points: Optional extras include history of art (with guided visits), literature and theatre courses.

**Institut Montarry -
Ecole de Langues en Oc**
210 avenue du Val de Montferrand
34090 Montpellier
Tel: 04 67 52 57 79
Fax: 04 67 52 31 26
Email: bjboyer101@aol.com

Hours/wk: 24-36
Price/wk (FF): 2100
Class size: 12
Min. stay: 1 week
Min. age: 15
Open: All year

Exams: DELF / DALF

Accommodation: Families or studios.

Special courses: Courses for teachers.

Other useful points: Courses by phone, internet study. Afternoons are spent on cultural activities, guided visits, conferences on painting, cinema etc.

International House
62, rue Gioffredo, 06000 Nice
Tel: 04 93 62 60 62
Fax: 04 93 80 53 09
Email: info@ih-nice.com
Web: http://www.ih-nice.com

Hours/wk: 20-35
Price/wk (FF): 2100-10,500
Class size: 4-10
Min. stay: 1 week
Min. age: 15
Open: 4th Jan-17th Dec. (1999)

Exams: DELF

Accommodation: Families, studios or hotels.

Special courses: French for business etc., work placements, courses for juniors and seniors.

Other useful points: Evening and weekend activities arranged. Self-study centre.

Institut Supérieur d'Etudes Francophones
Ombrosa International
95 quai Clémenceau
69300 Caluire
Tel: 04 78 23 22 63
Fax: 04 78 23 56 22

Hours/wk: 20-35
Price/wk (FF): 3500-4300
Class size: 4-12
Min. stay: 1-2 weeks
Min. age: 13-14
Open: Nov & Feb half-terms + Easter, July & Aug

Exams: Certificate of attendance only.

Accommodation: Half-board accommodation at the centre included in the price.

Other useful points: ISEF is located in an 11 hectare park with sports facilities.

International House - Montpellier
Espace Coural, 34000 Montpellier.
administrative address:
20 Passage Dauphine, 75006 Paris
Tel: 01 44 41 80 20
Fax: 01 44 41 80 21
Email: 106310.1071@compuserve.com
Web: http://www.ilcgroup.com/french/
montpellier.html

Hours/wk: 15
Price/wk (FF): from 2550
Min. stay: 2 weeks
Min. age: 12-15, 16-18, 18+
Open: Summer only

Accommodation: Full-board
accommodation with families or
residence included in the price.

Other useful points: Situated in 8
hectares of grounds with range of sports
including football, badminton and
volleyball. Beginners and advanced
levels NOT accepted.

IS Aix-en-Provence
9 cours des Arts et Métiers
13100 Aix-en-Provence
Tel: 04 42 93 47 90
Fax: 04 42 26 31 80
Email: is.aix@aix.pacwan.net
Web: http://www.is.se

Hours/wk: 15-26
Price/wk (FF): 1700-7100
Class size: 3-10
Min. stay: 2 weeks
Min. age: 18
Open: All year (except Christmas)

Exams: CCIP

Accommodation: Families, residences
or hotels.

Special courses: French for
commerce, courses for teachers.
Cookery or painting.

Other useful points: Multimedia
facilities. Activities and excursions, with
at least 1 social evening per week.

La Cité des Langues
116, rue Saint-Rose
73000 Chambéry
Tel: 04 79 33 89 89
Fax: 04 79 33 89 80
Email: lacitedeslangues@icor.fr

Hours/wk: 10-35
Price (FF): 2500/mth (at 20hrs/wk)
Min. stay: 1 week
Min. age: 17
Open: All year

Exams: DELF / DALF, CCIP & Alliance
Française

Accommodation: Families or studios

Special courses: French for business
and tourism

Other useful points: 1-1 tuition
available - price: 4000FF/wk for 35hrs.
Au-pair and work experience
placements arranged. Facilities include
a language laboratory and multimedia
room.

La Sabranenque
rue de la Tour de l'Oume
30290 Saint-Victor-la-Coste
Tel: 04 66 50 05 05
Fax: 04 66 50 12 48
Email: contact@sabranenque.com

Hours/wk: 15
Price (FF): 10,000-25,000
Class size: 2-7
Min. stay: 4 weeks
Min. age: 18-70
Open: Feb-May & Sept-Dec

Accommodation: Accommodation at
the school is included in the price.

Other useful points: Centre only deals
with 12 students at a time and has a
library and video room. Home cooked
meals, lots of activities and visits.

Languages Plus
Rue Pierre Devoluy
06000 Nice
Worldwide enrolment:
Tel: Canada: ++1 416 7117
Fax: Canada: ++1 416 5990
Email: info@LanguagesPlus.com
Web: http://www.LanguagesPlus.com

Hours/wk: 20-30
Price/wk (FF): On application
Class size: 8-12
Min. stay: 1 week
Min. age: 18-85
Open: All year

Exams: DELF / DALF

Accommodation: Families or foyers

Other useful points: Full programme
of cultural activities.

Langues Sans Frontières (L.S.F.)
3, Impasse Barnabé, 34000 Montpellier
Tel: 04 67 91 31 60
Fax: 04 67 91 31 61
Email: info@lsf.fr
Web: http://www.lsf.fr

Hours/wk: 15-30
Price/wk (FF): 1225-3160
Class size: 1-15
Min. stay: 1 week
Min. age: 11
Open: All year

Exams: DELF / DALF

Accommodation: Families, residence,
studios or hotels.

Special courses: Work placements
(internships), youth courses (11-18) in
Montpellier & Paris, exam preparation,
others on demand.

Other useful points: The school is
located in a 17th Century building in the
heart of Montpellier. Full programme
of sports & activities. Library.

Languazur sarl
22 Bd de la République
06400 Cannes
Tel: 04 93 39 02 90
Fax: 04 93 99 44 02
Email: 114054.2250@compuserve.com

Open: All year

Accommodation: Comfortable hotels.

Special courses: Socio-cultural
component

Other useful points: Aimed at
professional adults. The centre has just
changed management and no further
details are available at the time of going
to print. Contact them for latest
information.

Langueurop
30 rue de France
06000 Nice
Tel: 04 93 88 51 47
Fax: 04 93 88 11 62
Email: marietheresepelayo@compuserve.com

Hours/wk: 4½-30
Price/wk (FF): 750 (15hr/wk)
Class size: 3-10
Min. stay: 1 week
Min. age: 16
Open: All year (except Christmas)

Exams: DELF

Accommodation: Families, studios or hotels.

Special courses: French for business

Other useful points: All levels accepted. Museum visits and excursions.

Logos
2 Chemin des Marronniers
38100 Grenoble
Tel: 04 76 49 68 16
Fax: 04 76 70 03 24
Email: logos@isworld.com
Web: http://www.logos.fr

Hours/wk: 4-35
Price/wk (FF): 1400-11,000
Class size: 1-6
Min. stay: 10 hours
Min. age: 18
Open: 1st Jan-23rd Dec

Accommodation: Families, studios or hotels.

Special courses: All types tailor-made on request

Other useful points: Groups courses available if arranged in advance.

Linguarama Grenoble
Mini Parc Alpes Congrès
6 rue Roland Garros
38320 Eybens
Tel: 04 76 62 00 18
Fax: 04 76 25 89 60
Email: grenoble@linguarama.com
Web: http://www.linguarama.com

Hours/wk: 22½-42½
Price/wk (FF): On application
Class size: mostly 1-1 tuition
Min. stay: flexible
Open: All year

Accommodation: Families

Special courses: Available on request

Other useful points: All levels from beginners to advanced. Generally aimed at intensive executive courses. Lessons can start any day of the week, but you have to let the centre know 1wk before you arrive.

Lyon Langues
3, Grande rue des Feuillants, 69001 Lyon
Tel: 04 78 39 76 90 Fax: 04 78 30 18 46
Email: Lyon-Langues@wanadoo.fr

Hours/wk: 15-21
Price/wk (FF): 750-1100
Class size: 3-12
Min. stay: 2 weeks
Min. age: 16
Open: All year

Exams: DELF/DALF preparation courses.

Accommodation: Families, foyers, residences, studios, apartments or hotels.

Special courses: French for business, cultural courses, French for tourism.

Other useful points: Facilities include a library, video room and mediatheque. Cultural and sightseeing trips organised. Lyon Langues has been accredited by the 'OPQF', a professional organisation for training centres.

(see following page)

LYON LANGUES
3, Grande rue des Feuillants
69001 LYON
Tél: 04.78.39.76.90
Fax: 04.78.30.18.46
e-mail: Lyon-Langues@wanadoo.fr

"Lyon-Langues bénéficie du Label Qualité décerné par l'O.P.Q.F. (l'Office Professionnel de Qualification des organismes de Formation). Ce label est pour vous une garantie de compétence et d'efficacité"

Cours de langue française d'octobre à juin et de juillet à septembre (cours d'été)

● sessions de 2 semaines minimum
● 15 à 21 heures de cours de langue et civilisation française par semaine.

* Groupes de 12 personnes maximum.
* Hébergement (chambres d'étudiants, studios).
* Activités culturelles et touristiques. * Tous niveaux acceptés (débutants absolus à avancés). * Préparation aux unités des diplômes DELF et DALF. * Bibliothèque, médiathèque, vidéothèque. * Assistance pour toutes les démarches administratives en France.
* "Système échange langue / culture."
Pour plus d'informations contactez-nous.

Montpellier Espace Langues
1 bis, rue de Verdun
34000 Montpellier
Tel: 04 67 92 44 78
Fax: 04 67 92 44 78
Email: espace.langues@hol.fr

Hours/wk: 15
Price (FF): 40 per hour
Min. stay: 1 wk (summer), 1 sem (year)
Open: All year

Exams: DELF / DALF

Accommodation: Families or studios

Special courses: Available on demand

Other useful points: Facilities include a library and video room. Various workshops. Social evenings.

Millefeuille Provence
Château Correnson
30150 Saint-Geniès-de-Comolas
Tel: 04 66 50 46 63
Fax: 04 66 50 22 05
Email: rogues@millefeuille-provence.com
Web: http://www.millefeuille-provence.com

Hours/wk: 15 (approx.)
Price/wk (FF): On application
Class size: 5 max.
Min. stay: 1 week
Min. age: 18

Accommodation: Full-board accommodation at the centre

Other useful points: As well as standard language tuition the centre also offers a vocational business programme. This consists of: 5 hrs group tuition per week, 5 hours 1-1 tuition and 5 hours meeting local business people. Facilities include language lab, library and swimming pool.

Nova Langue
43, rue de l'Université, 34000 Montpellier
Tel: 04 67 60 92 09
Fax: 04 67 60 92 09
Email: novalangue@aol.com
Web: http://www.asian-way.com/nova

Hours/wk: 15-25
Price/wk (FF): 900-1700
Class size: 3-8
Min. stay: 1 week
Min. age: 17
Open: All year (except Christmas holidays)

Exams: DELF / DALF, CCIP

Accommodation: Families, residences or studios.

Special courses: French for business, secretaries and gastronomy. Courses for teachers.

Other useful points: Cookery courses, painting workshops, guided visits and a range of excursions and sports.

NOVALANGUE

The Mediterranean Way of Life
All year long

Located in the historical centre of Montpellier, a young and dynamic city (70,000 students), in the south of France next to the Mediterranean sea. Very involved teachers offering high quality and personalised teaching in a friendly atmosphere.

Courses: from 15 hours to 25 hours per week
• General French language courses, French for business, private teaching, evening classes.
• For students, teachers, businessmen.

New in 1999: Private classes for families or specific groups upon request.

Duration: From 1 week to 1 semester.

Exams: DELF, DALF, CCIP

Accommodation: in host families, students' flat or hotel residences.

Tuition fees: 4wks 3000 FF / 1 semester 7200 FF

Economic formula: *4 wks tuition + accommodation* 5800 FF (beginners) / 6800 FF (other levels)

43 rue de l'Université, 34000 Montpellier
Tel: +33 467 60 92 09
Fax: +33 467 60 92 09
Email: novalangue@aol.com
Web: http://www.asian-way.com/nova

NOVA LANGUE

Regency School of English & French
7 avenue Prince Pierre
98000 Monaco
Tel: (377) 92 05 21 21
Fax: (377) 92 05 27 29

Hours/wk: 15-30
Price/wk (FF): approx. 2100 (15hrs/wk)
Class size: 1-6
Min. stay: 1 week
Min. age: none
Open: All year (except Christmas holidays)

Exams: CCIP

Accommodation: Families or hotels.

Special courses: French for business.

Other useful points: 1-1 tuition and small private groups (e.g. family or friends) also arranged. Prices start at around 260FF/hr.

Pluriel Langues
213, Promenade des Anglais
06200 Nice
Tel: 04 93 97 16 73
Fax: 04 93 96 84 85
Email: PlurielLangues@compuserve.com
Web: http://ourworld.compuserve.com/homepages/PlurielLangues

Hours/wk: 15-30
Price/wk (FF): 1000-8300
Class size: 1-8
Min. stay: 1 week
Min. age: 16
Open: All year (except Christmas)

Exams: DELF, DALF, CCIP

Accommodation: Families, residence, studios or hotels.

Special courses: French for business, law and medical French.

Other useful points: Activities arranged by the school. Member of IALC (International Association of Language Centres)

Sud-Langue-Méditerranée
8 place de Comédie
34000 Montpellier
Tel: 04 67 66 30 11
Fax: 04 67 66 30 11
Email: contact@sudlangue.com
Web: http://www.sudlangue.com

Hours/wk: 15-20 + work
Price/wk (FF): 1300-2150
Class size: 1-9
Min. stay: 1 week
Min. age: 16
Open: All year

Exams: DELF / DALF, CCIP

Accommodation: Families, residence, studios or apartments.

Special courses: French for business, French cookery, literature workshops.

Other useful points: Library / newspaper room. Cultural activities, sports and excursions.

The Marzio School
7 rue des Baumes
13800 Istres
Tel: 04 42 55 16 82
Fax: 04 42 55 10 83
Email: marzio.school@aix.pacwan.net

Hours/wk: 2-60
Price/wk (FF): 600-18,000 (300/hrs)
Class size: 1-1 tuition only
Min. stay: 12 hours
Min. age: 18
Open: All year

Exams: DELF

Accommodation: Hotel

Special courses: Available depending on the needs of the students. The school specialises in business French.

Other useful points: The school is situated in a large industrial zone in Provence. Marseilles is 25mins away, Aix 35mins and Avignon 45mins.

UFCM - Société Européenne de Formation
1, rue de la Verrerie
06150 Cannes La Bocca
Tel: 04 92 19 40 40
Fax: 04 93 90 22 45
Email: ufcm@ufcm.com
Web: http://www.ufcm.com

Hours/wk: 15-30
Price (FF): from 4200/2wks
Class size: 8-10
Min. stay: 2 weeks
Min. age: 18
Open: All year

Accommodation: Families or apartments (half-board with family included in the price)

Other useful points: French + Skiing programme: Jan-March, 15hrs French + 10hrs ski instruction per wk = 12,500FF for 2 wks with shared apartment, ski pass, equipment and insurance. Language + work experience courses also offered.

Université d'Aix Marseille III -Institut d'Etudes Françaises pour Etudiants Etrangers
23, rue Gaston de Saporta
13625 Aix-en-Provence
Tel: 04 42 21 70 90 Fax: 04 42 23 02 64

Hours/wk: 8-20 (+ workshops)
Price (FF): 6000 semester, 9000 yr, 4800 for summer intensive.
Class size: 12-18
Min. stay: 1 month
Min. age: 18
Open: All year

Exams: CCIP

Accommodation: Families, studio or apartments. University residence during summer.

Special courses: French for business. Cookery, wine-tasting and French cinema.

Other useful points: Special courses for foreign diplomats available (7 hours day/ 4wks - price 15,000 FF). Optional excursions.

Université d'Avignon et des Pays du Vaucluse- Centre de Cours Internationaux d'Avignon
1 avenue Saint-Jean 84000 Avignon
Tel: 04 90 86 61 35 Fax: 04 90 85 08 08
Email: cassev@saturne.uni-avignon.fr
Web: http://www.univ-avignon.fr

Hours/wk: 15-25
Price/wk (FF): 1000 (or 7000 sem)
Class size: 10-20
Min. stay: 3 wks (summer)
Min. age: 18
Open: All year (except Aug)
Exams: DELF/ DALF

Accommodation: Families or residence.

Special courses: French for economics & commerce, for secretaries, courses for teachers.

Other useful points: Students can follow other courses at the university. They also benefit from the full range of on-campus facilities and activities.

**Université Catholique de Lyon -
Institut de Langue et de Culture
Françaises**
25, rue du Plat, 69288 Lyon Cedex 02
Tel: 04 72 32 50 53 Fax: 04 72 32 51 82
Email: ilcfLyon@ipl.fr

Hours/wk: 15-25
Price (FF): 3120/mth (summer), 5750/
10wks (during year)
Class size: 20-25
Min. stay: 1 month
Min. age: 18 (+ baccalaureate equivalent)
Open: All year

Exams: DELF / DALF, CCIP

Accommodation: Families, residences
or foyers

Special courses: French for business.
Courses for teachers.

Other useful points: 1 week's course
in Cannes during the film festival
(advanced levels only). Contact with
local families. Activities arranged
throughout the year.

**Université Lumiere-Lyon 2
Centre International d'Etudes
Françaises**
16, quai Claude-Bernard,
69365 Lyon Cedex 07
Tel: 04 78 69 71 35 Fax: 04 78 69 70 97
Email: Aliette.jeannez@univ-lyon2.fr
Web: http://signserver.univ-lyon2.fr/cief/ciel.html

Hours/wk: 4-18
Price (FF): 1500 (semester)- 2700/mth
(summer)
Class size: 10-25
Min. stay: 1 semester (1mth summer)
Min. age: 18
Open: All year

Exams: DELF / DALF, CPLF, DEF, DSEF

Accommodation: Families or
residences (summer only)

Special courses: French for business.
Courses for teachers.

Other useful points: Students can
attend some lectures. Excursions and
museum visits.

Université d'Eté de Menton
Office du Tourisme
BP 239
06506 Menton
Tel: 04 92 41 76 72
Fax: 04 92 41 76 82
Email: etienne.andre@cote-azur.cci.fr

Hours/wk: 20-25
Price/wk (FF): from 1300
Min. stay: 2 weeks
Min. age: 17
Open: July & August

Accommodation: Families or
residence

Special courses: Courses for teachers

Other useful points: Range of
workshops, including commerce,
theatre and cookery. Guided museum
visits. Students can also participate in
an end of course show!

Université de Nice Sophia-Antipolis
CAVEL
98 blvd Edouard Herriot
06204 Nice cedex 3
Tel: 04 93 37 53 83
Fax: 04 93 37 55 82

Hours/wk: 15
Price (FF): 4750 (semester)
Min. stay: 1 semester
Min. age: 18
Open: mid Oct to mid May

Other useful points: Emphasis is on
audio-visual learning, with 1 hour a day
spent in the language laboratory. All
levels accepted, even complete
beginners.

Université de Nice Sophia-Antipolis
Etudes Françaises pour l'Etranger
98 blvd Edouard Herriot
06204 Nice Cedex 3
Tel: 04 93 37 53 89
Fax: 04 93 37 54 98
Email: glenza@unice.fr

Hours/wk: 15-20
Price (FF): 3900 (semester)
Class size: 15-25
Min. stay: 1 semester
Min. age: 18
Open: mid Oct-mid June

Exams: DELF/ DALF, CPLF, DEF, DSEF

Special courses: Economics, management, literature. Courses for teachers.

Other useful points: Accompanied visits and excursions

Université de Perpignan
Université d'Eté
52 avenue de Villeneuve
66860 Perpignan Cedex
Tel: 04 68 66 60 50 Fax: 04 68 66 03 76
Email: ue@univ-perp.fr
Web: http://www.univ-perp.fr

Hours/wk: 24-36
Price/wk (FF): from 1350
Class size: 8-15
Min. stay: 2 weeks
Min. age: 16
Open: June-August

Exams: DELF / DALF, CCIP

Accommodation: Families, residences (on campus), studios or hotels.

Special courses: French for diplomacy, economics & commerce, tourism & hotels. Courses for teachers (various).

Other useful points: Language laboratory, study room & self-service video room. Organised activities and sports + weekend excursions.

Université Perpignan
Centre d'Etudes Françaises pour Etudiants Etrangers
52, avenue de Villeneuve
66860 Perpignan
Tel: 04 68 66 20 13 Fax: 04 68 66 20 19
Email: cef@univ-perp.fr
Web: http://www.univ-perp.fr

Hours/wk: 14-16
Price (FF): 3650 (semester), 6259 (year)
Min. stay: 1 semester
Min. age: 17
Open: Oct-May

Exams: CPLF, DEF, DSEF

Accommodation: Families, studios or apartments.

Other useful points: Beginners not accepted after the 2nd semester. Students can sit in on other lectures and benefit from the various campus activities available during the year.

Université de Provence
Service Commun d'Enseignement du
Français aux Etudiants Etrangers
29 avenue Robert Schuman
13621 Aix-en-Provence
Tel: 04 42 95 32 16 Fax: 04 42 20 64 87
Email: scefee@newsup.univ-mrs.fr
Web: http://newsup.univ_mrs.fr/
~wscefee/index.html

Hours/wk: 12-18
Price (FF): 4500 (semester), 7500 (yr)
Class size: 14-20
Min. stay: 1 semester
Min. age: 18
Open: 12th Oct - 21st May

Exams: DELF / DALF

Accommodation: None arranged but
can give contact addresses.

Special courses: General course +
options (e.g. history, art, cinema etc.)

Other useful points: Students can use
the 3 university libraries and other
facilities of the campus (sports,
restaurants etc.)

Université Paul Valéry, Montpellier III
IEFE, Route de Mende
34199 Montpellier Cedex 5
Tel: 04 67 14 21 01
Fax: 04 67 14 23 94

Hours/wk: 15-22
Price (FF): 5000 (semester),
4200 (mth-summer)
Class size: 16-20
Min. stay: 1 month (summer), 1
semester (yr)
Min. age: 18
Open: All year

Exams: DELF / DALF, CPLF, DEF, DSEF

Accommodation: University residence
(summer only)

Special courses: Courses for teachers

Other useful points: 1 month summer
courses July-Sept, with special all
inclusive rate of 7500FF.

Université de Savoie
ISEFE, BP 1104
73011 Chambéry Cedex
Tel: 04 79 75 84 14 Fax: 04 79 75 84 16
Email: isefe@univ-savoie.fr

Hours/wk: 15-20
Price/wk (FF): 480-1100
Class size: 8-16
Min. stay: 3 wks (summer) 15 wks (year)
Min. age: 18
Open: All year

Exams: DELF / DALF, CCIP, CPLF,
DEF, DSEF

Accommodation: Families, studios,
apartments, hotels + on site foyer /
residence in summer.

Special courses: French for business,
French for tourism.

Other useful points: University library
+ ISEFE library. Sports with French
students. Daily activities in summer,
weekly in winter. Skiing, rafting, cycling
etc + organised soirées.

Université Stendhal-Grenoble III
Centre Universitaire d'Etudes
Françaises
BP 25, 38040 Grenoble Cedex 9
Tel: 04 76 82 43 27 Fax: 04 76 82 43 90
Email: cuef@u-grenoble3.fr
Web: http://www.u-grenoble3.fr/cuef

Hours/wk: 16-25
Price/wk (FF): 885-1150
Class size: 12-20
Min. stay: 1 month
Min. age: 18
Open: All year

Exams: DELF / DALF, CCIP ,CPLF,
DEF, DSEF

Accommodation: Families, residences,
foyers, studios or hotels.

Special courses: French for business,
tourism and hotels. Courses for
teachers.

Other useful points: Self-service
language laboratory, video & computer
rooms. Use of the university library and
other campus facilities.

**Université du Temps Libre
des Alpes du Sud
Cours d'Eté pour Etudiants Etrangers**
rue Bayard
05000 Gap
Tel: 04 92 51 38 94
Fax: 04 92 53 98 31
Email: utl.gap@wanadoo.fr
Web: http://perso.wanadoo.fr/utl.gap/

Hours/wk: 15
Price/wk (FF): 1100
Class size: 10-15
Min. stay: 1 week
Min. age: 17
Open: 12th July - 20th Aug (1999 dates)

Exams: Centre's own certificate.

Accommodation: Families, foyers, studio, apartments or hotels.

Other useful points: Various sports available: rafting, hiking, rock-climbing, mountain biking etc.

5 SOUTH WEST FRANCE

La Rochelle, formerly an isolated rocky island, is a very beautiful port with a rich historical past.
Once the stronghold of Protestants, it incurred the wrath of Richelieu and paid dearly for its love of Free-thinkers. For three centuries it was amongst the first ports to establish trade links with the new world, the *Musée du Nouveau Monde* being a testimony to this glorious and adventurous past.

Bordeaux is the elegant capital of this wine producing region. Excellent museums, attractive buildings and a thriving student community combine to make Bordeaux an interesting city for both residents and visitors.

Arcachon is a beach resort which is home to the highest sand dune in Europe. This pleasant little town enjoys good weather and is famous for its oyster and pleasure boating.

Pau, nestled in the Pyrenees, offers breath taking views of the mountains. It has a mild climate, beautiful parks and a relaxed atmosphere.

Toulouse, the fourth largest city in France, stands firmly at the foot of the Pyrenees. This busy, lively city is an important cultural centre and one in four inhabitants is a student. It is also home to many high-tech industries, with modern buildings blending with old Florentine style ones.

AVERAGE TEMPERATURES FOR THE SOUTH WEST (°C):

Jan / Mar Apr / Jun   Jul / Sep Oct / Dec

---

10 / 12   18 / 24   26 / 23   19 / 10

 LOW COST ACCOMMODATION:

Auberge de Jeunesse -
Ile de Bourgines, 16000 Angouleme
49 FF per night (bed only)
TEL: (05) 45 92 45 80 FAX: (05) 45 95 90 71

Auberge de Jeunesse -
87, avenue de Bordeaux, 33970 Cap Ferret
30 to 44 FF per night (bed only)
TEL: (05) 56 60 64 62

Auberge de Jeunesse - avenue des Minimes,
BP 305, 17013 La Rochelle Cedex
68 FF per night (with breakfast)
TEL: (05) 46 44 43 11 FAX: (05) 46 45 41 48

Auberge de Jeunesse (Pau) - 'Logis des Jeunes',
Base de Plein Air, 64110 Gelos
49 FF per night (bed only)
TEL: (05) 59 06 53 02

DIRECTORY OF COURSES IN THIS REGION

A Lot of French
Belair, 46120 Le Bouyssou
Tel: 05 65 40 92 82
Fax: 05 65 40 98 80
Email: info@a-lot-of.com
Web: http://www.a-lot-of.com

Hours/wk: 15-60
Price/wk (FF): 6000-15,000
Class size: 1-4
Min. stay: 5 days
Min. age: 10
Open: All year

Accommodation: Accommodation at the centre included in the price.

Special courses: Wine tasting courses, regional cookery, art.

Other useful points: Specialises in tailor-made language courses for companies and individuals, as well as translating and interpreting work.

Ateliers Linguistiques du Tarn (ALT)
"Fiolles", route de Montans
81600 Brens / Gaillac
Tel: 05 63 57 69 67
Fax: 05 63 57 65 22
Email: langues.loisirs81alt@wanadoo.fr
Web: http://www.fle.fr/alt

Hours/wk: 18-40
Price/wk (FF): 2900-3200
Class size: 1-6
Min. stay: 1 week
Open: All year

Exams: DELF / DALF

Accommodation: Residence (included in the price)

Special courses: History and literature.

Other useful points: ALT is located in a renovated farmhouse, by the bank of the river Tarn. Sports offered include cycling, canoeing and volleyball.

Alliance Française Toulouse
9 place du Capitole
31000 Toulouse
Tel: 05 61 23 41 24
Fax: 05 61 23 05 51

Hours/wk: 4-16
Price/wk (FF): 1900/mth (16hrs)
Class size: 6-16
Min. stay: 1 month
Min. age: 16
Open: All year

Exams: DELF and Alliance Française

Accommodation: Families

Other useful points: Self-service language laboratory. Range of workshops, including cinema, theatre and cookery. Excursions and social evenings.

BLS
1 cours Georges-Clemenceau
33000 Bordeaux
Tel: 05 56 51 00 76
Fax: 05 56 51 76 15
Email: bls@imaginet.fr
Web: http://www.bls-bordeaux.com

Hours/wk: 15-30
Price/wk (FF): 1350-5850
Class size: 2-8
Min. stay: 1 week
Min. age: 17
Open: All year

Exams: DELF / DALF, CCIP

Accommodation: Families, studios, apartments or hotels.

Special courses: French for business + a 'wines of Bordeaux' course.

Other useful points: The school has a garden and a common-room for the students. *(see following page)*

Intensive French in Bordeaux

Independent Private Further Education Establishment recognised by the Rectorate of Bordeaux.

- ● ● Beautiful location.
- ● ● Top quality programs for students, businessmen, diplomats.
- ● ● Mini groups (4-8 per. max.)
- ● ● Bordeaux Wine Course.
- ● ● Biarritz Summer Program for teenagers.
- ● ● High standard accommodation.

BLS   1 cours Georges Clemenceau
33000 Bordeaux - France
tel: 33 5 56 51 00 76 fax: 33 5 56 51 76 15
e-mail: bls@imaginet.fr

CCI de Bayonne
Centre d'Etudes des Langues
50-51 allées Marines, BP 215
64102 Bayonne
Tel: 05 59 46 58 16
Fax: 05 59 46 59 70

Hours/wk: 20
Price (FF): 2500/2wks
Min. stay: 2 weeks
Min. age: 18
Open: Summer

Exams: CCIP

Accommodation: Families, studios or hotels.

Special courses: French for secretaries, hotels / tourism.

Other useful points: Preparation for CCIP, 'Certificat de français du secrétariat' and the 'Certificat de français du tourisme et de l'hôtellerie'.

CAREL
48, Bd Franck Lamy, BP 219C
17205 Royan
Tel: 05 46 39 50 00
Fax: 05 46 05 27 68
Email: info@carel.org
Web: http://www.carel.org

Hours/wk: 25
Price/wk (FF): 2600
Class size: 15 max.
Min. stay: 2 weeks
Min. age: 18
Open: All year

Exams: DELF / DALF

Accommodation: Families, residences, studios, apartments, hotels

Special courses: Courses for teachers

Other useful points: 4 language laboratories, TV studio, multimedia lab + mediatheque with videos, satellite TV & CD-ROMS. Activities arranged throughout the year.

Centre d'Etude des Langues
2 place de la Bourse
33076 Bordeaux
Tel: 05 56 79 51 80
Fax: 05 56 51 98 79
Email: cel.gicfo.bordeaux@wanadoo.fr

Hours/wk: 4-20
Price/wk (FF): 2850 / 40hrs
Class size: 3-7
Min. stay: 40 hours
Min. age: 18
Open: All year

Exams: Examen Européen (in April)

Accommodation: Hotels

Special courses: French for business, tourism, restaurants and wine courses.

Other useful points: Self-study centre with books, videos, CD-ROM etc.

sent email
5/25/99

POITIERS UNIVERSITY

ROYAN CITY COUNCIL

STUDY FRENCH ON THE ATLANTIC COAST SOUTHWEST FRANCE

The CAREL, a multicultural centre accredited by the University of Poitiers, welcomes French adult students and foreign students.
Open all year.
Communicative approach for oral expression and aural comprehension - Language laboratory sessions - Multimedia resource center - TV studio. Exceptional multimedia facilities.

GENERAL FRENCH / ADULT COURSES

. Intensive courses (25 sessions/ week)
. 2 weeks minimum - 3, 6, 12 months
. Levels: complete beginners to advanced

DELF / DALF

. Possibility to sit all DELF / DALF units over a 3-month stay.

REFRESHER COURSES FOR TEACHERS

This programme aims at creating innovative material for the class and at updating information about current teaching methods.

JUNIOR PROGRAMME

. For 12-17 year olds.
. Combines language training with cultural and sports activities.

Accommodation guaranteed.
Permanent hospitality - service and social programme.

ROYAN: North of Bordeaux - 4 hours by train from Paris - near international airport -
Sandy beaches - quiet and safe seaside resort - a region rich in Roman and Romanesque architecture and known for its vineyards and sea-food.

CAREL (EURPAG) BP 219 C 17205 ROYAN Cedex FRANCE
Phone: (33) 5 46 39 50 00   Fax: (33) 5 46 05 27 68
E-Mail: info@carel.org   http://www.carel.org

Cetradel
Immeuble "Les Portes de Bègles"
A Quai Wilson
33130 Bègles
Tel: 05 57 35 53 55
Fax: 05 57 35 53 50
Email: cetradel@wanadoo.fr
Web: http://www.cetradel-france-langue.com

Hours/wk: 15-30
Price/wk (FF): 2200-12,600
Class size: 1-6
Min. stay: 1 week
Min. age: 18
Open: All year

Accommodation: Families or hotels.

Special courses: French for business, finance, law and telecommunications.

Other useful points: Immersion programme: 'language and wine".

Institut d'Etudes Françaises pour Etrangers (IEFE)
Faculté des Lettres
BP 1160
64013 Pau
Tel: 05 59 92 32 22
Fax: 05 59 92 32 65
Email: suee.messv1@univ.pau.fr

Hours/wk: 14-20
Price/wk (FF): 3000-4900
Class size: 10-24
Min. stay: 1 term
Min. age: 18
Open: Sept - July

Exams: CPLF, DEF, DSEF

Accommodation: Families, foyers, residences, studios, apartments, hotels

Special courses: Commercial French

Other useful points: Students can use all the facilities of the campus.

Eurocentre
Parc de la Francophone
Avenue Marillac
17024 La Rochelle Cedex 01
Tel: 05 46 50 57 33
Fax: 05 46 44 24 77
Email: lar-info@eurocentres.com
Web: http://www.eurocentres.com

Hours/wk: 20-25
Price (FF): 6400 /4wks
Class size: 10-15
Min. stay: 2 weeks
Min. age: 16
Open: All year (except Christmas)

Exams: CCIP

Accommodation: Families

Special courses: French for business, tourism, cookery & wine.

Other useful points: Self-service language laboratory, computer & video room. Organised excursions.

Institut Universitaire de Langue et de Culture Françaises -
Institut Catholique de Toulouse,
Fac libre des Lettres
31, rue de la Fonderie, BP 7012
31068 Toulouse cedex 07
Tel: 05 61 36 81 30 Fax: 05 61 25 82 75
Email: iscam@iscam.unisoft.fr
Web: http://195.101156.65/région/ict/iscam/iscam.htm

Hours/wk: 3-20
Price (FF): 5500/semester (20hrs)
Class size: 6 min
Min. stay: 1 month
Min. age: 16 (with parental permission)
Open: All year

Exams: DELF / DALF

Accommodation: Families, foyers or residences.

Other useful points: 3 mth summer courses from July-Sept: 20hrs/wk = 3000FF. Conversation and phonetics workshops. Cultural excursions in and around Toulouse.

La Ferme -
Centre Linguistique Residentiel
La Petite Eguille, 17600 Saujon
Tel: 05 46 22 84 31 Fax: 05 46 22 91 38
(in winter tel/fax: 01 46 67 73 31)
Email: fer@filnet.fr
Web: http://www.edunet.com/laferme

Hours/wk: 15-25
Price/wk (FF): 6500-9500
Class size: 1-5
Min. stay: 1 week
Min. age: 18
Open: May to Oct

Accommodation: Accommodation at the centre and meals are included in the price.

Other useful points: Reductions available if 2 students of the same level enrol at the same time and are prepared to study together. Price range then 5500-7600FF/wk Also, 1-1 tuition available all year in Paris. Courses held anywhere: your hotel, in a café or even in a park!

Université de Poitiers
Institut d'Etudes Françaises
102, rue de Coureilles
Les Minime, 17024 La Rochelle Cdx 1
Tel: 05 46 51 77 50 Fax: 05 46 51 77 57
Email: ief@ief-la-rochelle.fr

Hours/wk: 20-30
Price/wk (FF): 1670-2375
Class size:
Min. stay: 2 weeks
Min. age: 18
Open: All year

Exams: DELF / DALF, CCIP + own certificates

Accommodation: Families, residences (summer only) or studios.

Special courses: French for business, commerce & economics, literature, civilisation. Courses for teachers.

Other useful points: Contact with French speakers arranged. Wide range of excursions and free conferences.

Université de la Rochelle
CUFLE (Centre universitaire de français langue étrangère)
Faculté des Langues, Arts et Sciences Humaines
Parvis Fernand Braudel
17071 La Rochelle cedex 9
Tel: 05 46 45 68 00 Fax: 05 46 50 59 95
Email: pgrange@flash.univ-lr.fr
Web: http://www.univ-lr.fr/flash/p1.html

Hours/wk: 5-15
Price/wk (FF): See below
Class size: 20 max
Min. stay: 2 weeks
Min. age: 18
Open: Sept-Nov

Exams: DELF

Other useful points: Courses are free for students enrolled for at least 1 semester at the university. They can choose from 2 week intensive courses, with 15hrs tuition per week and activities in the afternoon, or from semester courses of 5-8hrs wk, which run parallel with academic courses.

Université de Toulouse- Mirail
Dépt. d'enseignement du FLE
5 allée A. Machado, 31058 Toulouse Cdx
Tel: 05 61 50 45 10 Fax: 05 61 50 41 35
Email: defle@univ-thse2.fr
Web: http://www.univ-tlse2.fr

Hours/wk: 15-21
Price (FF): 1000/25wks during yr, from 2800/mth (summer)
Class size: 10-20
Min. stay: 1 mth (summer)
Min. age: 18 (+ equiv. of baccalaureate)
Open: All year

Exams: DELF / DALF, CPLF, DEF, DSEF, CCIP

Accommodation: Families or residences.

Special courses: French for business. Courses for teachers.

Other useful points: 1 month summer courses July-Sept. Academic year courses run from Nov-end of May. Students can participate in the activities and events organised by the university.

Université Michel de Montaigne-Bordeaux III
DEFLE, Domaine Universitaire
33405 Talence Cedex
Tel: 05 56 84 50 44 Fax: 05 56 84 51 05
Email: defle@montaigne.u-bordeaux.fr
Web: http://www.defle.montainge.u-bordeaux.fr

Hours/wk: 14-16
Price (FF): 2630 (semester)
Class size: 16-20
Min. stay: 1 semester
Min. age: 18 (+ equiv. of baccalaureate)
Open: Oct to June

Exams: DELF / DALF, CCIP, CPLF, DEF, DSEF

Accommodation: University residence (for exchange students only)

Special courses: Wide range of options: business, history, literature etc

Other useful points: Students benefit from the full range of university activities and facilities.

6 WESTERN FRANCE

Normandy is the land of pastoral beauty, famous for its butter, cream, cheese and cider.

Rouen, the largest city in Normandy, has a late gothic cathedral, many old churches, picturesque half-timbered houses and fine museums. It is an excellent base for visiting the region, whose attractions include Monet's house in Giverny.

Brittany's way of life is strongly influenced by the sea, which is never far away. Its coast of sandy beaches and spectacular cliffs, its charming old towns and strange megalithic sites, make Brittany an excellent region to visit.

Rennes, Brittany's capital, is an elegant if somewhat formal university town, home to some 40 000 students. It comes to life in July during the 'Tombées de la Nuit' festival, when the old town is transformed back to medieval times, with costumes, theatre and music.

Nantes, only 56 kilometres from the Atlantic coast, is an orderly city with a beautiful cathedral and splendid Ducal Palace. The botanical garden and Fine Art Museum are amongst the many attractions Nantes has to offer.

Angers, home of the largest tapestry in the world, 'the Apocalypse of St. John', is a delightful town. As expected, it has a castle (which took a century to build) and a cathedral with 13th century stained-glass windows.

Poitiers, further south, boasts a 12-13th century cathedral and many Romanesque churches. It has a strong cultural tradition with a large university. Poitiers has recently been pushed into the 20th century thanks to the opening of Futuroscope, a huge futuristic complex which attracts visitors from around France. Its new addition has put Poitiers on the map as one of France's most innovative cities.

AVERAGE TEMPERATURES FOR THE WEST (° C):

Jan / Mar	Apr / Jun	Jul / Sep	Oct / Dec
9 / 11	17 / 23	25 / 21	16.6 / 9.5

(Note: Normandy tends to be a few degrees colder)

 LOW COST ACCOMMODATION:

Auberge de Jeunesse -
'Port Beaulieu', 9 bd Vincent Gâche, 44200 Nantes
49 FF per night (bed only)
TEL: (02) 40 12 24 00 FAX: (02) 51 82 00 05

Auberge de Jeunesse -
1, Allée Roger Tagault, 86000 Poitiers
49 FF per night (bed only)
TEL: (05) 49 58 03 05 FAX: (05) 49 37 25 85

Auberge de Jeunesse -
10-12, Canal St. Martin, 35700 Rennes
49 FF per night (bed only)
TEL: (02) 99 33 22 33 FAX: (02) 99 59 06 21

Auberge de Jeunesse -
'Patrick Varangot', 37 avenue du R.P.Umbricht, BP 108,
35407 St.Malo Cedex.
68 FF per night (with breakfast)
TEL: (02) 99 40 29 80 FAX: (02) 99 40 29 02

A ➡ Z DIRECTORY OF COURSES IN THIS REGION

Alliance Franciase
79 quai du Havre, 76000 Rouen
Tel: 02 35 98 55 99 Fax: 02 38 89 98 58
Email: Alliance.francaise.Rouen@wanadoo.fr

Hours/wk: 5-20
Price (FF): from 32/ hr
Class size: 10-20
Min. stay: Variable
Open: All year

Exams: DELF and Alliance Française

Accommodation: Families, studios or hotels.

Special courses: French for business (1 wk intensive course with 20 hrs 1-1 tuition + half-board accommodation with family for 10,304FF)

Other useful points: Library, language laboratory and video room. Museum visits and a range of social activities.

CEFA Normandie / Centre d'Etudes de Lisieux
10,12, 14, Bd Carnot, BP 4176
14104 Lisieux Cedex
Tel: 02 31 31 22 01 Fax: 02 31 31 22 21
Email: centre.normandie@wanadoo.fr
Web: http://perso.wanadoo.fr/
centre.normandie

Hours/wk: 15-32
Price/wk (FF): 2486
Class size: approx. 12
Min. stay: 1 week
Min. age: 15
Open: 22nd March- 12th Nov (1999)

Exams: DELF / DALF and CPLF

Accommodation: Accommodation with families or residences included in the price.

Special courses: French for business.

Other useful points: Established in 1975. The centre is near Deauville and Paris. Sports available in the area include riding, tennis & golf. The centre organises 1 excursion each week.

CEL St. Malo
BP 6, St. Jouan-des-Guerêts
35430 St. Malo
Tel: 02 99 19 15 46 Fax: 02 99 81 48 78

Hours/wk: 20-25
Price/wk (FF): from 1560
Class size: 12 max.
Min. stay: 2 weeks
Min. age: 16
Open: July and Aug

Accommodation: Families, youth hostels, studios or hotels.

Special courses: French + cookery, French for business.

Other useful points: Tuition + accommodation packages: 20/hrs courses/wk + family accommodation = 5020FF for 2 wks. Students have free access to the multimedia facilities. Company visits plus various excursions and social evenings.

Centre International des Langues et Cultures
2, rue Mélusine
85240 Foussais-Payre
Tel: 02 51 51 45 34
Fax: 02 51 51 45 58

Hours/wk: 15-30
Price/wk (FF): 1300-1500
Class size: 8-20
Min. stay: 1 week
Min. age: 16
Open: All year

Accommodation: Families or residences

Special courses: Courses for teachers

Other useful points: FOR PRE-ARRANGED GROUPS ONLY! Not open to individuals.

Centre International d'Etudes des Langues (CIEL)
Rue du Gué Fleuri
BP 35, 29480 Le Relecq Kerhoun
Tel: 02 98 30 57 57 Fax: 02 98 28 26 95
Email: info@ciel.fr
Web: http://www.ciel.fr

Hours/wk: 20-30
Price (FF): 2900 (2 weeks)
Class size: 5-15
Min. stay: 2 weeks
Min. age: 16
Open: All year

Exams: DELF, CCIP & Alliance Française

Accommodation: Families, residences or hotels.

Special courses: French for business, tourism, secretaries, teachers.

Other useful points: Various workshops available in July & August. Multimedia centre, video-room, CD-ROMs and self-service language laboratory.

Château de Bellevue
49520 Le Bourg d'Iré
Tel: 02 41 61 51 42
Fax: 02 41 61 56 18
Web: http://www.fle.fr/bellevue

Hours/wk: 15
Price/wk (FF): 2100
Class size: 12 max.
Min. stay: 2 weeks
Min. age: 5-14 max.
Open: All year (groups), summer / Easter (individuals)

Accommodation: Full board accommodation at the centre is included in the price.

Other useful points: Situated in 25 hectares of grounds, the centre has its own ponies, tennis courts and small theatre. French children also attend the centre. Lessons take place in the morning, activities in the afternoon.

Centre International d'Etudes Françaises
Université Catholique de l'Ouest
3 place André Leroy, BP 808
49008 Angers Cedex 1
Tel: 02 41 88 30 15 Fax: 02 41 87 71 67
Email: cidef@uco.fr
Web: http://www.uco.fr/cidef

Hours/wk: 15-25
Price (FF): 4000/mth, 8400 (semester)
Class size: 12-24
Min. stay: 3 weeks
Min. age: 16
Open: All year

Exams: DELF / DALF, CCIP, Alliance Française (exam centre)

Accommodation: Families, residences (summer) or foyers.

Special courses: French for business, tourism and hotels. Courses for teachers.

Other useful points: Summer courses carry credits for US, Canadian & Japanese students. Chance to speak to French students every week.

Demos Langues
7, rue Guépin
44000 Nantes
Tel: 02 40 89 53 13
Fax: 02 40 89 50 92
Email: langues@demos.fr
Web: http://www.demos.fr

Hours/wk: ½-40
Price/wk (FF): On application
Class size: 1-6
Min. stay: 10 hours
Min. age: 11
Open: All year

Special courses: French for business. Business life in France.

Other useful points: Part of 'Groupe Demos' which has over 25 years experience in business training.

Ecolangues
11 rue de la Rame
49100 Angers
Tel: 02 41 25 73 73
Fax: 02 41 25 05 55
Email: ecolangues@francemultimedia.fr

Hours/wk: 10-50
Price/wk (FF): 1100-6000 (mini-grps)
Class size: 1-6
Min. stay: 1 week
Min. age: 18
Open: All year

Accommodation: Families or hotels.

Special courses: French for business, tourism and courses for teachers.

En Famille in Brittany
5 Impasse Pré Gerno
22190 Plérin
Tel: 02 96 73 18 68
Email: frogrman_cr@aol.com

Hours/wk: 12 hrs max
Price/wk (FF): 900 FF/12hrs
Class size: 1
Min. stay: 1 week
Min. age: 13
Open: All year

Accommodation: Families (1200FF per week)

Other useful points: 1-1 tuition or small groups. Specialises in teaching teenagers preparing for French exams. English, Dutch and Afrikaans spoken.

Ecole des Roches
BP 710, Avenue Desmolins
27137 Verneuil-sur-Avre
Tel: 02 32 23 40 21
Fax: 02 32 32 25 28

Hours/wk: 18-25+ (see below)
Price (FF): 9830/ 3wks
Min. stay: 3 wks
Min. age: 11-18 (some for adults)
Open: All year

Exams: DELF / DALF

Accommodation: At the centre included in the price.

Special courses: Courses for teachers

Other useful points: 60 hectare campus with restaurant, language laboratory, computer room etc. 1-10 mth total immersion courses with 18-25 hrs tuition + sports and workshops. Price = 9579FF/mth (with accommodation).

Espace Langues - Chambre de Commerce
4, rue Bisson
BP 90517, 44105 Nantes Cedex 4
Tel: 02 40 44 42 00
Fax: 02 40 73 63 06
Email: i.leflem@nantes.cci.fr
Web: http://www.nantes.cci.fr/cifoe

Hours/wk: 8-20
Price/wk (FF): 200-1500
Class size: 6-12
Min. stay: 1 week
Min. age: 16
Open: All year

Exams: DELF / DALF

Accommodation: Families, residences or studios.

Special courses: French for business, tourism and teachers.

Other useful points: Work experience can be arranged. Multimedia language laboratory and resource centre.

Inlingua Normandy
Technosite des Bruyeres
8 rue Jean Rostand
76140 Le Petit Quevilly
Tel: 02 35 69 81 61 Fax: 02 35 69 81 59
Email: inlrouen@normandnet.fr
Web: http://www.inlingua.fr/rouen

Hours/wk: 15-35
Price/wk (FF): variable
Class size: 1-10
Min. stay: 1 week
Min. age: 10
Open: All year

Exams: DELF / DALF

Accommodation: Families, residence, studios, apartments, hotels.

Special courses: French for business, French & Cookery, French & Gastronomy

Other useful points: Self-study multimedia centre. Activities & excursions every week. Airport transfers.

Maison des Langues
1, place du Maréchal Juin
35000 Rennes
Tel: 02 99 30 25 15
Fax: 02 99 30 34 54

Hours/wk: 10-30
Price/wk (FF): 1350 (20hrs)
Class size: 4-6
Min. stay: 1 week
Open: All year

Accommodation: Families, foyers, studios or hotels.

Special courses: French for business, law and hotels/tourism. Courses for teachers.

Other useful points: Self-service audio/video room. Range of excursions and social evenings.

Langue et Communication
16, rue de Penhoët
35065 Rennes cedex
Tel: 02 99 78 15 62
Fax: 02 99 79 33 91
Email: langue_et_communication@wanadoo.fr

Hours/wk: 6-23
Price/wk (FF): 885 (15 hrs)
Class size: 10 max
Min. stay: 1 week
Min. age: 17
Open: All year

Exams: DELF / DALF

Accommodation: Families, youth hostels, camping or hotels.

Special courses: French for business, commerce, law and tourism. Courses for diplomats and teachers.

Other useful points: Mini work placements arranged. Combination group / 1-1 courses offered: 10 hrs (grps) + 10 hrs (1-1) costs 4800FF / wk.

Service Universitaire des Etudiants Etrangers - Université de Nantes
rue de la Censive du Tertre
BP 81227, 44312 Nantes cedex 3
Tel: 02 40 14 10 26
Fax: 02 40 14 13 10
Email: cefle@humana.univ-nantes.fr

Hours/wk: 6-20
Price/wk (FF): 150-300
Class size: 25
Min. stay: 3 weeks
Min. age: 18
Open: All year (except 1st 2wks of Aug)

Exams: DELF/ DALF, CPLF, DEF, DSEF

Accommodation: Families, foyer, residence, studio or hotels.

Other useful points: Library, theatre workshop and cultural excursion.

St Brelade's Institut
4 place Boisouze
35400 St Malo
Tel: 02 99 81 28 45
Fax: 02 99 21 01 94

Hours/wk: 15-22 1/2
Price/wk (FF): 2750-7100
Class size: 2-5-10
Min. stay: 1 week
Min. age: 12
Open: All year

Exams: DELF / DALF

Accommodation: Families, apartments or hotels

Special courses: French for business

Other useful points: Price includes accommodation with a host family (hotels & apartments extra). Easter/ Summer visits and excursions at no extra cost.

Université de Caen
Centre d'Enseignement Universitaire International pour Etrangers, BP 5186, Esplanade.de la Paix, 14032 Caen Cdx
Tel: 02 31 56 55 38 Fax: 02 31 93 69 19
Email: ceuie@admin.unicaen.fr
Web: http://www.unicaen.fr/unicaen/ service/ceuie

Hours/wk: 20-27
Price (FF): 1850/3wks, 7500 (1 year)
Class size: 8-20
Min. stay: 3 weeks
Min. age: 18 (+ equiv. of baccalaureate)
Open: Sept-May

Exams: DELF / DALF, CCIP, CPLF, DEF, DSEF

Accommodation: Families

Special courses: French for business, economics, literature, translations. Courses for teachers.

Other useful points: Conferences, debates and French cinema. European study courses also available. Use of university facilities.

Université de Caen
Cours Internationaux d' Eté
BP 5186, 14032 Caen cedex
Tel: 02 31 56 55 38
Fax: 02 31 93 69 19
Email: ceuie@admin.unicaen.fr
Web: http://www.unicaen.fr/unicaen/ service/ceuie

Hours/wk: 25
Price (FF): 3000 (2 wks)
Class size: 8-25
Min. stay: 2 weeks
Min. age: 18
Open: June-Aug

Accommodation: Families or university residence.

Other useful points: All levels accepted. Range of social events.

Université de Poitiers
Centre de Français Langue Etrangère
95 av. Recteur Pineau
86022 Poitiers
Tel: 05 49 45 32 94 Fax: 05 49 45 32 95
Email: centre.fle@cri.univ-poitiers.fr

Hours/wk: 18-25
Price (FF): 4800/yr. 2800/3wks (summer)
Class size: 15-25
Min. stay: 3wks (summer), 1 sem. (yr)
Min. age: 18 (yr), 16 (summer)
Open: All year (except Aug)

Accommodation: University residence (summer). List of addresses given during year.

Special courses: Courses for teachers

Other useful points: Summer courses (July & Aug) consist of 21 hours of tuition plus 4 hours of language and cultural workshops. Excursions and activities are included in the price for July.

Université de Rennes 2
CIREFE
6 av. Gaston Berger
35043 Rennes Cedex
Tel: 02 99 14 13 00
Fax: 02 99 14 13 10
Email: cirefe@uhb.fr
Web: http://www.uhb.fr/cirefe

Hours/wk: 18-20
Price (FF): 5000 (26 wks)
Class size: 15-30
Min. stay: 1 academic year
Min. age: 18 (+ equiv. of baccalaureate)
Open: Oct - May

Exams: CPLF, DEF, DSEF

Accommodation:

Special courses: On demand

Other useful points: Beginners not accepted. Students have access to multimedia facilities. Various cultural excursions related to the course.

Université de Rennes 2
Haute Bretagne
Cours Universitaire d' Eté de St. Malo
6, ave Charles Tillon
35044 Rennes Cedex
Tel: 02 99 14 10 92
Fax: 02 99 14 10 95
Email: jean-francois.bouillard@uhb.fr
Web: http://www.uhb.fr

Hours/wk: 15
Price/wk (FF): 1000
Class size: 10-15
Min. stay: 2 weeks
Min. age: 16
Open: July to August

Accommodation: Families

Other useful points: 3 weekly excursions arranged. Also guided visits and social evenings.

7 CENTRAL FRANCE

This region groups together the eastern part of the Loire Valley and the Massif Central, two areas which differ greatly, yet both possess their own beauty.

Tours has the reputation for being the town where the purest French is spoken. It is a very pleasant town, often referred to as a miniature Paris, and makes a good base for exploring the many châteaux found in this region. A lively student population ensures a good nightlife, most of which is centred around the Place Plumereau in the heart of the old town.

Amboise is a town nestled under its most impressive, fortified château. Though rich in history, it has retained much of the traditional flavour of a small, provincial French city. Leonardo da Vinci lived the last three years of his life in Amboise, in a manor house called Le Clos Lucé. It now houses an exhibition of some of his inventions, constructed using his original notes.

Vichy, a well known spa resort in the Massif Central, is a very pretty town which has retained much of its glamour from its heydays of 'La Belle Époque.' The Grand Casino, the Opera House and large park have ensured that Vichy is still a great favourite with both French and foreign visitors. As an added bonus, this smart town offers excellent water sport facilities.

St. Etienne is an industrial city, but has a very lively cultural life. Amongst its many museums is the superb Museum of Modern Art, whilst younger visitors will enjoy a trip to the Planetarium. With its large open spaces and plenty of sunshine, St. Etienne is a modern city which has not forgotten its past.

AVERAGE TEMPERATURES FOR CENTRAL FRANCE (°C):

Jan / Mar	Apr / Jun	Jul / Sep	Oct / Dec
8 / 10	16 / 24	26 / 22	16.5 / 7.5

 LOW COST ACCOMMODATION:

Auberge de Jeunesse -
18, rue de l'Hôtel Pasquier, Les Grouets, 41000 Blois
40 FF per night (bed only)
TEL: (02) 54 78 27 21

Auberge de Jeunesse - Centre Animation Accueil,
rue Descartes, BP 233, 37500 Chinon
46 FF per night (bed only)
TEL: (02) 47 93 10 48 FAX: (02) 47 98 44 98

Auberge de Jeunesse - 'Cheval Blanc',
55, avenue de l'URSS, 63000 Clermont-Ferrand
46 FF per night (bed only)
TEL: (04) 73 92 26 39 FAX: (04) 73 92 99 96

Auberge de Jeunesse (Saint-Etienne) - 'Le Pertuiset',
Les Echandes, 42240 Unieux
30 to 44 FF per night (bed only)
TEL: (04) 77 35 72 94

Auberge de Jeunesse - 'Parc de Grandmont',
avenue d'Arsonval, 37200 Tours
46 FF per night (bed only)
TEL: (02) 47 25 14 45 FAX: (02) 47 48 26 59

A ➤ Z DIRECTORY OF COURSES IN THIS REGION

Alliance Française du Val de Loire
21 place Saint-Martin, 41100 Vendôme
Tel: 02 54 73 13 20
Fax: 02 54 73 23 20
Email: alliance.francaise@mail.dotcom.fr
Web: http://www.mygale.org/08/afvdl/

Hours/wk: 4-20
Price/wk (FF): 200-1900 (see below)
Class size: small groups
Min. stay: 1 week
Open: All year

Exams: Alliance Française

Accommodation: Families or hotels.

Special courses: French for business.

Other useful points: Summer immersion courses offered: 20/hrs wk + extensive range of activities in a group of 8 max = 4800FF/ 2wks.

CCI Auxerre (CEL)
26 rue Etienne-Dolet
89015 Auxerre cedex
Tel: 03 86 49 40 00
Fax: 03 86 49 40 09

1-1 tuition or in-company training. Courses over the telephone also offered.

Candidates prepared for the Certificat Européen.

CAVILAM
14, rue Marechal Foch, 03206 Vichy cdx
Tel: 04 70 58 82 58
Fax: 04 70 58 82 59
Email: 106112.1000@compuserve.com
Web: http://www.cavilam.com

Hours/wk: 22
Price/wk (FF): 1330
Class size: 10-15
Min. stay: 1 week
Min. age: 16 (12 in July/Aug)
Open: All year

Exams: DELF / DALF, CCIP

Accommodation: Families, residences, studios or hotels.

Special courses: French for commerce/economics, tourism/hotels. Courses for teachers.

Other useful points: All inclusive junior courses (age 12+) in July/Aug: 2wks with 15hrs tuition per wk + sports and full-board accommodation = 7300FF/ mth (July) or 6980FF in Aug.

Centres International d'Etudes Françaises de Touraine
Château Bois Minhy
41700 Chemery - Contres
Tel: 02 54 79 51 01
Fax: 02 54 79 06 26

Hours/wk: 24
Price/wk (FF): 3400-3700
Class size: 4
Min. stay: 2 weeks
Min. age: 18-80
Open: Jan-Nov

Exams: Alliance Française

Accommodation: Price includes accommodation at the Château.

Special courses: Gastronomy

Other useful points: Situated in 7 hectares of grounds, the centre is ideal for students who enjoy nature and outdoor activities. Makes good base for exploring the château of the Loire.

...re Linguistique pour Etrangers
7-o, Place du Châteauneuf
37000 Tours
Tel: 02 47 64 06 19 Fax: 02 47 05 84 61
Email: herve@cle.fr
Web: http://www.cle.fr

Hours/wk: 20
Price/wk (FF): from 1680
Class size: 7 max
Min. stay: 1 week
Min. age: 18
Open: All year

Exams: DELF

Accommodation: Families, studios, apartments or hotels.

Special courses: Available as 1-1 tuition (330FF / hr)

Other useful points: Self-access language laboratory, library, video-room, CD-ROMS and internet. Weekly excursion.

Eurocentre
9 Mail St Thomas, BP 214
37402 Amboise Cedex
Tel: 02 47 23 10 60
Fax: 02 47 30 54 99
Email: info@eurocentres.com
Web: http://www.eurocentres.com

Hours/wk: 20-25 (+options)
Price/wk (FF): 1475-1675 (+see below)
Class size: 10-15
Min. stay: 3 weeks
Min. age: 16 (summer 12)
Open: All year

Exams: DELF

Accommodation: Families (945 FF/ wk)

Other useful points: Special children's courses (age 12+) during summer. Price: 9483 FF / 3 weeks / full-board accommodation with families. Conferences and excursions, plus sports during the summer.

Ecole des Trois Ponts
Château de Matel
42300 Roanne
Tel: 04 77 71 53 00
Fax: 04 77 70 80 01
Email: info@3ponts.edu
Web: http://3ponts.edu

Hours/wk: 19-25
Price/wk (FF): from 4900
Class size: 6 max
Min. stay: 1 week
Min. age: 18-80
Open: May-Nov.

Accommodation: Full-board accommodation at the school is included in the price.

Special courses: French for business.

Other useful points: The school is located in large grounds with a private pool. Bicycles are lent to students.

Institut de Touraine
1 rue de la Grandière, BP 2047 / EP
37020 Tours Cedex
Tel: 02 47 05 76 83
Fax: 02 47 20 48 98
Email: Institut.Touraine@wanadoo.fr
Web: http://www.institut-touraine.asso.fr

Hours/wk: 19-25
Price (FF): 10,500/3mths (yr), 4750/mth (summer)
Class size: 15/16
Min. stay: 2 weeks (Easter & summer)
Min. age: 16
Open: All year
Exams: DELF / DALF, CCIP

Accommodation: Families, residences, apartments or hotels.

Special courses: French for business, tourism, hotels, restaurants and secretaries. Courses for teachers.

Other useful points: Library, mediatheque and multimedia facilities. Organised excursions and activities.

Saint-Denis European School
19 avenue du gal de Gaulle, BP 146
37601 Loches Cedex
Tel: 02 47 59 04 26
Fax: 02 47 94 04 50
Email: euroschool@saint-denis.net
Web: http://www.saint-denis.net

Hours/wk: 15-20
Price/wk (FF): 1000-1200
Class size: 10-15
Min. stay: 2 weeks
Min. age: 12
Open: All year (except Christmas)

Accommodation: Families, residence or hotels.

Special courses: Executive courses on demand

Other useful points: Academic year programme for students (including IGCSE). Sports & cultural activities in summer. Language laboratory, multimedia room and library.

Université Blaise Pascal
Service Universitaire des Etudiants Etrangers, 34 avenue Carnot
63006 Clermont-Ferrand Cedex 1
Tel: 04 73 40 64 97
Fax: 04 73 40 62 83
Email: suee@univ-bpclermont.fr
Web: http://www.univ-bpclermont.fr

Hours/wk: 15
Price (FF): 3000 (semester), 5500 (year)
Min. stay: 1 mth (summer), 1 semester (during year)
Min. age: 18
Open: All year

Exams: DELF / DALF, CPLF, DEF, DSEF

Accommodation: Residences, foyers or studios

Other useful points: Beginners not accepted in the summer. Conferences, theatre workshop, cinema and excursions.

Université de François Rabelais
CUEFEE - Bureau des Etudes Etrangers, BP 4103
37041 Tours Cedex
Tel: 02 47 36 66 53
Fax: 02 47 36 67 25
Web: http://www.univ-tours.fr/etra5.htm

Price (FF): 3400 for academic year
Min. stay: academic year
Min. age: 18 (with equiv. of baccalaureate)
Open: Oct - May

Exams: DSEF

Other useful points: For advanced levels only (the course prepares for the DSEF). Half of the course is spent on language instruction and the other half on French culture (history, society, literature, cinema etc..) Various visits and theatre trips organised during the year.

Université Jean-Monnet -
Centre International de Langue
et Civilisation
30 rue Ferdinand Gambon
Site Gambon A, 42100 Saint-Etienne
Tel: 04 77 46 32 00 Fax: 04 77 46 32 09
Email: chalabi@univ-st-etienne.fr
Web: http://www.univ-st-etienne.fr

Hours/wk: 5-25
Price/wk (FF): 190-980
Class size: 8-15
Min. stay: 1 academic yr (1 wk in summer)
Min. age: 16
Open: All year
Exams: DELF / DALF

Accommodation: Families, residences or foyers.

Special courses: French for commerce/economics and hotels. Courses for teachers.

Other useful points: Summer courses July to Sept: 15hrs/wk = 675FF. Facilities include a language laboratory, computer & video rooms. Students can participate in improvised theatre & radio broadcasts.

Université d'Orléans
Programmes Internationaux
Service des Affaires Internationales
BP 6749
45067 Orléans Cedex 2
Tel: 02 38 41 71 5
Fax: 02 38 41 72 55
Email: Programmes.Internationaux@univ-orleans.fr
Web: http://www.univ-orleans.fr

Hours/wk: 20-25
Price (FF): 4600 (1month)
Min. stay: Variable
Min. age: 18
Open: All year

Accommodation: Families, residences or studios

Special courses: Courses for teachers

Other useful points: 1 month summer course in July for individuals. Otherwise, during rest of year courses organised to suit the demands of companies or educational institutions.

CORRESPONDENCE COURSES

Learning French at home is a good way of building your confidence before going to France, or of maintaining your skills after a visit. The following pages contain comprehensive details of courses offered by the CNED. For further details, contact the centre directly:

CENTRE NATIONAL D'ENSEIGNEMENT À DISTANCE (CNED)

Téléport 4, BP 200
86980 Futuroscope cedex
TEL: 05 49 49 94 94
FAX: 05 49 49 96 96
E-MAIL: accueil@cned.fr
WEB: http://www.cned.fr

The CNED (National Centre for Distance Learning) is the leading supplier of French language distance learning programmes in the world. It operates under the control of the French Ministry of Education, providing a wide range of courses, including French as a foreign and second language.

 General Course Information:

• Minimum age is 16 years old.

• You have 10 months to complete your course, but do not have to stick to a pre-set timetable for handing in your work (i.e. you study at your own pace within those 10 months). However, those preparing for the DAEFLE have a more rigid work schedule.

- The study materials will reach you approximately 2 weeks after your enrolment.

- Two types of tariffs: The lower is for individuals paying for their course, the higher price for cases where your company pays for part or all of your course.

- NB: Enrolment in a course does not mean that you will sit an exam. Should you wish to take an exam at the end of your course, you will have to make the arrangements yourself (contact your nearest French consulate for a list of recognised examination centres in your country).

 Study Materials:

For each course you will be supplied with:

- A study manual with exercises and answers
- Audio cassettes with exercises and answers
- A work book for your written assignments

You will also be able to take part in internet forums. In addition to these materials, some courses include video tapes and extra audio cassettes, enabling you to send in your oral exercises for correction.

 GENERAL LANGUAGE COURSES

Français pour débutants anglophones

Level required at start: Complete beginner / near beginner
Approx. Study Time: 120 hours
Objective: To cope with simple everyday situations in French (both written & orally). Helps to start prepare for DELF 1st level, units A1 & A2.
Format / Price: 4 written assignments and 4 oral assessments (1220FF - 2425FF)

Entraînement à la communication orale

Level required at start: Beginner (120-150hrs of French)
Approx. Study Time: 60 hours
Objective: To gain an intermediate level in spoken French.
Helps to prepare for units A1 & A2 of the DELF 1st level.
Format / Price: 3 written assignments and 3 oral assessments (805FF - 1850FF)

Perfectionnement en langue et culture

Level required at start: Advanced beginner (200-300hrs of French)
Approx. Study Time: 120 hours
Objective: To improve written & oral expression/comprehension. Helps to prepare for units A1, A2, A3 and A4 of the DELF 1st level.
Format / Price: 6 written assignments and 4 oral assessments (1245FF - 2425FF)
Includes a video tape.

Perfectionnement en communication écrite

Level required at start: Intermediate (200-400hrs of French)
Approx. Study Time: 120 hours
Objective: To improve written comprehension, writing skills and grammatical knowledge.
Helps to prepare for all written parts of the DELF 1st level.
Format / Price: 8 written assignments (1060FF - 2690FF)

Français écrit pour l'université / DALF

Level required at start: Advanced intermediate (500-600hrs of French)
Approx. Study Time: 150 hours
Objective: To perfect written comprehension and writing skills in order to study at a French university. Provides intensive preparation for units B1 and B3 of the DALF.
Format / Price: 10 written assignments (1060FF - 2690FF)

Français oral pour l'université / DALF

<u>Level required at start:</u> Advanced intermediate (500-600hrs of French)
<u>Approx. Study Time:</u> 150 hours
<u>Objective:</u> To perfect oral comprehension and expression in order to study at a French university. Helps to prepare for units B2 and B4 of the DALF.
<u>Format / Price:</u> 3 written assignments and 7 oral assessments (1060FF - 2690FF)
Includes a video tape.

 FRENCH FOR WORK

Specialist courses are offered for those who have to use French for their work. All require an intermediate level of French (around 200hrs of tuition). The courses all consist of 7-10 written assignments with an estimated study time of 120 hours. They cost 1060FF - 2700FF each and come with a video tape.

- **Français de la gestion et du commerce**
- **Français du droit**
- **Français de la médecine**
- **Français, langue diplomatique**

 COURSES FOR TEACHERS OF FLE

Several courses for teachers, or prospective teachers, of French as a foreign language are available, the main one being the DAEFLE:

- **DAEFLE (Diplôme d'aptitude à l'enseignement du français langue étrangère de l'Alliance Française)**

Diploma preparation course, with 12 written assignments. Study time of approx. 720 hours. Before enrolment candidates must pass an Alliance Française test (contact your nearest AF branch). Price: 11,000 - 20,400FF

Other courses for teachers:

- **Perfectionnement linguistique et méthodologique** (120hrs - 6 written & 4 oral assignments - 1245 FF- 2425 FF)

- **Linguistique appliquée à l'enseignement du FLE**
- **Didactique générale du FLE**
- **Phonétique et pédagogie de la prononciation**
- **Méthodologie de l'enseignement de la grammaire**
- **Méthodologie de l'enseignement de la civilisation et de la littérature**
- **Observation et guidage de classe**

The above courses all last around 120 hours, have 2 written assignments (no orals) and cost 2000 - 3400 FF.

 ALLIANCE FRANÇAISE COURSES

The Alliance Française has temporarily suspended their distance learning programmes, but they should be running again by the middle of 1999. For the latest details contact:

M. le Responsable des cours par correspondance
Alliance Française, 101 Bd Raspail, 75270 Paris Cdx 06.
TEL: 01 45 44 38 28 FAX: 01 45 44 89 42
E-Mail: info@paris.alliancefrançaise.fr

EXAMS

Language exams not only enable you to provide evidence of your abilities, but also present a useful goal for you to achieve during your stay, providing an incitement to learn.

Below, you will find most of the major exams open to foreign students. Once you have decided on the type of exam that is best suited to your requirements (i.e. on your level of French, amount of time you will study for the exam, any preferences made by your employers/ educational establishment) you should check to see:

a) if your language school offers preparation for the exams
b) when you will be able to sit the exam.

Most schools would also be able to offer you help and guidance if you are unsure.

CHAMBRE DE COMMERCE ET D'INDUSTRIE DE PARIS (C.C.I.P.)

Certificates and Diplomas awarded by the
Paris Chamber of Commerce

Chamber of Commerce exams take place in Paris and 60 centres around France, as well as in 610 centres in nearly 90 countries world-wide.

To obtain the address of your nearest centre, and exact examination dates, contact:

Chambre de Commerce et d'Industrie de Paris,
Service des Examens pour étrangers,
28 rue de l'Abbé-Grégoire,
75279 Paris Cedex 06 France.
Fax: (01) 49 54 28 90
Email: examdfda@ccip.fr

Certificat de Français du Tourisme et de l'Hôtellerie

- 360 hours of French
- Exam consists of 8 tasks:
  - 2 written comprehensions [eg.multiple choice] (1hour)
  - 2 written papers [eg. letter, telex] (1hour)
  - 2 listening comprehensions (45 mins)
  - 2 orals [eg.role play] (30 mins)
- Dates: January, June, December
- Fee: 525 FF

Certificat de Français des Professions Scientifiques et Techniques

- 360 hours of French
- Exam consists of 8 tasks:
  - 2 written comprehensions (1 hour)
  - 2 written papers [eg. letters] (1 hour)
  - 2 listening comprehensions (45 mins)
  - 2 orals [eg. reading aloud, interview] (30 mins)
- Dates: January, June, December
- Fee: 525 FF

Certificat de Français du Secrétariat

- 360 hours of French
- Exam consists of 8 tasks:
  - 2 written comprehensions (1 hour)
  - 2 written papers [letter, message, telex] (1 hour)
  - 2 listening comprehensions [eg. note taking] (45 mins)
  - 2 orals [eg. role play] (30 mins)
- Dates: January, June, December
- Fee: 525 FF

Certificat de Français Juridique

- 480 hours of French
- Exam consists of 8 tasks:
    2 tests - multiple choice & varied exercises (1hour)
    2 written comprehensions (1 hour)
    2 written papers [eg.letters, faxes] (1hour)
    2 orals - [eg. role play] (20 mins)
- Dates: January, June, December
- Fee: 525 FF

Certificat Pratique de Français Commercial et Economique

- 480 hours of French
- Exam consists of 6 tasks:
    Test [multiple choice, fill in blanks etc] (1 hour)
    Reading comprehension [answer questions on,
    produce summary] (1 hour)
    Correspondence [letter writing] (45 mins)
    Translation [into and from mother tongue] (1 hour)
    Oral [interview] (15 mins)
    Oral [translation into French from text in mother-
    tongue] (15 mins)
- Dates: January, April, June, July, August, September,
- December
- Fee: 420 FF

Diplôme Supérieur de Français des Affaires

- 600 hours of French
- Exam consists of 10 tasks:
    Essay [on a current economic issue] (1½ hours)
    Questionnaire [8-15 questions on commerce] (1 hour)
    Correspondence [letter] (1 hour)
    Translation [into French] (45 mins)
    Dictation [25-30 lines from newspapers] (45 mins)
    Oral [on socio-economics] (15 mins)
    Oral [on commerce] (15 mins)

Oral [translation into French] (15 mins)
Oral [translation into mother tongue] (15 mins)
Oral [résumé of a text & interview] (15 mins)
- Dates: January, June, December
- Fee: 525 FF

Diplôme Approfondi de Français des Affaires

- 720 hours of French
- Candidates must hold the Diplôme Supérieur
- Exam consists of:
    Writing of an in-depth paper on a commercial or
    economic subject
    Supporting the work in front of a panel of examiners
    (research must be carried out under the supervision
    of a CCIP approved teacher)
- Fee: 840 FF

Test d'Evaluation en Français (TEF)

- New test which assesses the fluency of non-native speakers.

- Tests GENERAL language skills (i.e. not just business related).

- Provides candidates with a performance score. It is not a diploma or certificate. (Similar to TOEFL)

- Testifies the candidate's command of French when they apply to Grandes Ecoles, universities, companies etc.

- Consists of 3 sections: Listening comprehension, written comprehension and structure & vocabulary - 150 multiple choice questions in total - duration 2hrs 30mins.

- Also 2 optional sub-tests: Written or oral expression.

- Dates for 1999: 23/1, 19/3, 7/5, 19/6, 29/10 and 4/12

- Fee: 250 FF + 200 FF for each optional section

MINISTERE DE L'EDUCATION NATIONALE
D.E.L.F & D.A.L.F

Diplomas awarded by the French Ministry
of National Education.

The French Ministry of National Education awards two diplomas, the DELF and the DALF. The exams take place both in France and abroad. For details contact your nearest French consulate.

Diplôme d'Etudes de Langue Française (D.E.L.F.)

The DELF is divided into two levels:

* Level I - containing four units (A1 to A4)

* Level II - containing two units (A5 to A6)

Units can be taken individually in any order, and once passed a credit is given which remains valid indefinitely.

The Level II DELF is only open to candidates who have passed Level I.

Candidates who obtain the DELF level I should be able to understand and make themselves understood in a wide variety of everyday situations in a French-speaking environment.

Candidates with the DELF level II will be able to operate in a more specialised area of interest (eg. economics or another academic domain).

<u>Unit Objectives and Exam Contents:</u>

<u>Level I</u>
  - **Unit A1: General**

General Objective: To understand and express oneself on simple topics related to everyday situations.

Exam contents: Listening comprehension (15 mins); oral (role play - 15 mins); 2 written papers (letter & short essay 60-100 words, 30 mins each).

  - **Unit A2: Ideas and Feelings**

General Objective: To understand and express feelings, intentions, opinions, points of view and arguments.

Exam contents: 2 orals each lasting 10 mins *(or at the discretion of the Chief Examiner 1 oral and 1 listening comprehension)*; reading comprehension (30 mins); written paper (120-160 words, 30 mins)

  - **Unit A3: Reading and Essay Writing**

General Objective: To understand the content and function of simple written texts and to write letters of the type required in daily life.

Exam contents: Oral (on a given text - 15 mins); reading comprehension (45 mins); written paper (eg. job application letter - 45 mins)

  - **Unit A4: Linguistics**

General Objective: To use the linguistic systems (phonetic, prosodic & morpho-syntactic) with a high degree of accuracy. The emphasis of this unit is on linguistic competence as opposed to communication skills.

Exam contents: Listening comprehension (3 or 4 exercises) and oral (30 mins); Written comprehension and essay (1 hr 30 mins)

Level II

- ## Unit A5: Culture and Civilisation

General Objective: To understand and discuss in general terms the main features of certain cultural and socio-cultural aspects of contemporary France and of the francophone world, and to identify those features which contrast with aspects of contemporary Britain (or your country).

The candidate chooses one of six topics: Work, Institutions, Travel, Contemporary Society, Study or Modern Civilisation.

Exam contents: 2 orals (presentation of a text + discussion - 10 mins each); reading & writing (read text of 500-700 words on chosen topic and write a summary - 1 hr 30 mins).

- ## Unit A6: Specialised Subjects

General Objective: To understand a text related to the candidate's field of special interest or profession and to discuss its contents.

The candidate chooses one of four topics: Life Sciences (including the environment and ecology); Economics and Law; Social and Human Sciences; Mathematics, Physics and Technology.

Exam contents: Oral (report and discuss contents of text related to chosen field - 2 tests of 10 mins)

Diplôme Approfondi de Langue Française (D.A.L.F.)

The DALF is made up of four units (B1 to B4).
As with the DELF, credit units are permanently valid.

Candidates are expected to demonstrate their ability to use French in both general and specialist contexts. However, whilst candidates are expected to engage in a fairly technical discussion of their chosen field, the test is one of language and not of specialist knowledge.

In order to sit the DALF exams, candidates must have a level II DELF or (in the U.K.) a pass at French GCE 'A' level. (For other recognised awards, contact your local consulate.) It is also possible to take a DALF access test.

> *Candidates who pass the DALF are deemed to be exempt from the language requirement for entry to French universities and to be able to follow a course in their chosen field.*

Unit Objectives and Exam Contents:

- **Unit B1: Written Comprehension**

General Objective: To understand all aspects of an authentic published text on a general topic and to write detailed answers to a number of questions related to the text.

Exam contents: Reading and Writing (résumé of text, answers to 5 questions related to the text) Total time given - 2 hours 15 mins. Length of text to be studied - 500-700 words.

- **Unit B2: Oral Comprehension**

General Objective: To understand all aspects of an authentic spoken discussion on a general topic recorded on audio or video tape.

Exam contents: Listening comprehension (résumé of the recorded text or answering questions on it). Time given - 30 mins max.

- **Unit B3: Written Comprehension of Specialised Subject**

General Objective: To understand all aspects of a selection of authentic published texts in the special field chosen and to write detailed answers to a number of questions related to the texts.

Candidates select one of six topics: Law, Economics, Social Sciences, Human Sciences, Life Sciences or Mathematics & Physics.

Exam contents: Reading and Writing (résumé of text, answers to 5 questions related to the text) Total time given - 2 hours 15 mins. Length of text to be studied - 500-700 words.

- **Unit B4: Oral Comprehension of Specialised Subject**

General Objective: To make an oral presentation on a topic related to the special field chosen for unit B3, to answer questions, and to participate in broader discussion.

Exam contents: Oral (presentation of topic + discussion) Time given - 40 mins (plus 1 hr 20 mins for preparation.)

UNIVERSITY DIPLOMAS

Certificates and Diplomas awarded by French Universities.

In addition to various internal diplomas, most French universities grant foreign learners of French the following qualifications:

- Le Certificat Pratique de la Langue Française (1st level) - CPLF

- Le Diplôme d'Etudes Françaises (2nd level) - DEF

- Le Diplôme Supérieur d'Etudes Françaises (3rd level) - DSEF

In order to sit the exams, candidates must have the equivalent of the French baccalaureate ('A' levels, high school leaving diploma).

Some French universities allow students with a DSEF to access the second year of the DEUG (a two year university course, similar to a mini-degree.) Contact individual universities for further details.

ALLIANCE FRANÇAISE (A.F.)

Certificates and Diplomas awarded by
the Alliance Française

 GENERAL FRENCH:

Certificat Elémentaire de Français Pratique (C.E.F.P.) - Level I

• Beginner's level French - 125 hours of tuition
(end of AF level I)
• Test consists of 5 sections:
  Written comprehension (30 mins)
  Essay writing (30 mins)
  Listening comprehension (20 mins)
  Oral test (10 mins)
  Grammatical test (20 mins)
• Exams take place every month
• Exam fees - 170 FF (or 300 FF if not an Alliance Française candidate)

Certificat Elémentaire de Français Pratique (C.E.F.P.) - Level II

• Intermediate level French - 250 hours of tuition
(end of AF level II)
• Test consists of 5 sections:
  Written comprehension (20 mins)
  Essay writing (40 mins)
  Listening comprehension (10 mins)
  Oral test (10 mins)
  Grammatical test (20 mins)
• Exams take place every month
• Exam fees - 170 FF (or 300 FF if not an Alliance Française candidate)

Diplôme de Langue (D.L.)

• Advanced level French - 400 hours of tuition
(end of AF level III)
• Test consists of 5 sections:
    Written comprehension (65 mins - 3 tasks of 40 mins,
    15 mins & 10 mins)
    Essay writing (45 mins)
    Grammatical test (45 mins)
    Listening comprehension (20 mins)
    Oral test (15 mins)
• Approved by the Ministry of National Education
• Exams take place in February, April, June, August, October
and December
• Exam fees - 390 FF (or 500 FF if not an Alliance Française
candidate)

Diplôme Supérieur d'Etudes Françaises Modernes (D.S.)

• Superior level French - 600 hours of tuition
(end of AF level IV)
• Test consists of 5 sections:
    Written comprehension and Essay writing -
    2 options: literature or civilisation (3 hrs 30 mins)
    Listening comprehension and oral test -
    2 options: literature or civilisation (20 mins)
    Grammatical test (1 hr 15 mins)
    Dictation (30 mins) and Summary (1 hr 45 mins)
• Approved by the Ministry of National Education
• Exams take place in February, April, June, August, October
and December
• Exam fees - 390 FF

Diplôme de Hautes Etudes Françaises (D.H.E.F.)

- Mastery level French - 900 hours of tuition
(end of AF level V)
- Test consists of 4 sections:
      Written comprehension and essay writing (4 hrs)
      Oral test (30 mins)
      Grammatical test (2 hrs 30 mins)
      Dictation (30 mins)
- Approved by the Ministry of National Education
- Exams take place in April, June and December
- Exam fees - 370 FF (1 option) 530 FF (2 options)

 FRENCH FOR SPECIAL PURPOSES:

Certificat Pratique de Traduction (C.P.T.)

- Advanced level French - 600 hours of tuition
(end of AF Commercial Translations level I)
- 3 language options: English - French, Spanish - French,
German - French.
- Test consists of 2 mains sections: Written & Oral.
      Written section: translation into French of a business
      letter (1 hr), translation into mother tongue of a press
      article (1 hr), résumé of a press article into French
      (1 hr 30 mins).
      Oral section: Translation into French and French to
      mother tongue translation of a press article and
      business letter. Lasts 15 mins plus preparation time.
- Exams take place in January and June
- Exam fees - 350 FF

Diplôme de Traducteur Commercial (D.T.C.)

• Superior level French - 900 hours of tuition
(end of AF Commercial Translations level II)
• 3 language options: English - French, Spanish - French, German - French.
• Test consists of 2 mains sections: Written & Oral.
> *Written section:* translation into French of a business letter (1 hr), translation into mother tongue of a press article (1 hr), résumé of a press article into French (1 hr), comprehension of mother tongue text (questions & answers in French).
> *Oral section:* Translation into French and French to mother tongue translation of a press article. Review of a mother tongue text in French.
• Exams take place in January and June
• Exam fees - 480 FF

Diplôme Supérieur d'Etudes Commerciales en Langue Française (D.S.E.C.)

• Superior level French - 600 hours of tuition
(end of AF level I of French for Business)
• Test consists of 4 sections:
> Grammatical test (45 mins)
> Knowledge of business affairs (1hr 45 mins)
> Written comprehension and essay writing (1 hr)
> Listening comprehension and oral test (20 mins)
• Approved by the Ministry of National Education
• Exams take place in May, June, August and December
• Exam fees - 350 FF

INTERNET SITES

The internet provides a vast array of language learning resources. It is possible to use on-line dictionaries, complete grammar exercises or get into contact with other language learners, so that you can exchange ideas and information.

One of the first sites you should look at is, of course, the Europa Pages home page. The address is:

http://www.europa-pages.co.uk/

You will find some of the information contained in this book, as well as details of other European language courses. Many of the links below are also provided on our site.

(Please note: In the fast moving world of the internet, it is likely that some of the site addresses given will have changed by the time you try to access them. Most should contain, however, a link to the new site.)

 Sites with lots of links to other French web pages

France and Francophonie: General information, internet resources etc. http://fllc.smu.edu/languages/French.html

The French Connection: Internet links to places and items of interest with a French theme. It is designed for students of French and francophiles in general.
http://www.anu.edu.au/french/french.html

Hapax: French Resources on the Web: http://hapax.be.sbc.edu

The Human Languages Page: http://www.june29.com/HLP

Language Learning Resource Centre: http://ml.hss.cmu.edu/llrc

Languages On-Line
http://www.knowledge.co.uk/xxx/mpcdir/online.htm

Multilingual Circus: http://www.multilinguals.com.au

Tennessee Bob's Famous French Links!
Useful guide to hundreds of sites on the language and
country. http://www.utm.edu/departments/french/french.html

Volterre - Resources for teachers and learners of French
http://www.wfi.fr/volterre

 Dictionaries

ARTFL Project: French-English Dictionary Form
Look up words in a simple French to English Dictionary
containing about 75,000 terms.
http://humanities.uchicago.edu/forms_unrest/FR-ENG.html

English-French Dictionary of Common Computing Terms
http://www.css.qmw.ac.uk/CSS/foreign/eng-french.html

French to English Dictionary
http://humanities.uchicago.edu/forms_unrest/FR-ENG.html

The Internet Dictionary Project
Multi-lingual dictionary - English to a wide range of other
languages. http://www.june29.com/IDP/IDPsearch.html

Language and Grammar

Argot Français - French slang dictionary
http://www.argots.com

CIEP : Testez vos connaissances
On-line French test from the Centre International d'Etudes
Pédagogiques.   http://www.ciep.fr/tester

Des Exercices de Grammaire - Test for teachers and their
students. Answers given immediately.
http://www.cssh.qc.ca/coll/profenligne/exercices1.html

Etienne French Educational Music
Songs to help students remember their verbs and grammar!
http://www.in.on.ca/~dwhite/etienne/index.html

Exercices de Français
Interactive site, testing grammar, dictation skills and more!
http://pages.infinit.net/jaser2

Foreign Languages for Travellers Basic phrases, vocabulary etc.
http://www.travlang.com/languages

France à la Carte
Educational site from the French Embassy in London
http://www.francealacarte.org.uk

French for Travellers- Basic French complete with audio-clips.
http://insti.physics.sunysb.edu/~mmartin/languages/french/
french.html

French Lessons from Everywhere
Links to loads of on-line French courses.
http://globegate.utm.edu/french/globegate_mirror/
frlesson.html

French Slang Short - Introduction to French slang words,
with pronunciations
http://www.easynet.co.uk/home/fslang.htm

French Verb Conjugation from the ARTFL Project. Conjugation of French verbs into most tenses. http://humanities.uchicago.edu/forms_unrest/inflect.query.html

Glossary of French information technology terms. Searchable site, in French. http://www-rocq.inria.fr/~deschamp/CMTI/glossaire.html

Glossary of Internet Terms - English to French translations and explanations of technical terms. http://www.culture.fr/culture/dglf/internet.htm

Testez vos Connaissances en Français - Test of vocabulary and grammar. http://www.mygale.org/04/yhwh/test.htm

Verb Conjugation - Conjugate a verb by selecting the tense and entering the infinitive form of the verb in the box. http://humanities.uchicago.edu/forms_unrest/inflect.query.html

 Travel and Tourism

Allostop: Ride matching service to help backpackers travel around France. http://www.ecritel.frllostop/

Budget Travel - For travellers who don't want to pay 5 starprices! A central location for travel information world-wide. http://www.budgettravel.com

Eurotrip - A travel resource for budget independent travel in Europe. http://www.eurotrip.com

Excite City Net - Large database of tourist information for cities world-wide. http://www.city.net

FranceScape: Information to help plan a trip to France. Festivals, Specialised travel agents, tour operators etc. http://www.france.com/francescape/top.html

French Connections: French holiday catalogue, featuring privately owned gites, villas, farmhouses and apartments, plus useful information about France, updated regularly.
http://www.webconnection.co.uk

French Government Tourist Office:
http://www.francetourism.com/

French Travel Gallery: Information on France, including the WTA Hotel Reservation Centre to set-up hotel reservations.
http://www.bonjour.com/wta/

Leeds Good Value Guide to Paris Restaurants: Find three course meals with wine for as little as 100 FF.
http://www.wfi.fr/leeds/

Loire Valley: Information on the Loire Valley, including chateaux, wine production and tourism.
http://people.mne.net:1234/7217/LOIRE.HTM

Maison de la France: Over 1000 pages about France, including cities, monuments, festivals, sports and cultural activities. The site is in French and English.
http://www.franceguide.com/

Météo-France Weather Report: Today's weather and satellite pictures. Updated daily.
http://www.meteo.fr/tpsreel/e_tpsre.html

Paris, My Love: contains travel experiences, tips, and money saving ideas shared by numerous lovers of Paris.
http://members.aol.com/layout1/parislove

Ski France: promotion body of the French Ski Resorts Mayors Association; provides information on resorts, weather, lessons. http://www.skifrance.fr/

Tourism in France: Tourist guide about Paris and France.
http://www.w3i.com/

Tourisme en France: Large database on tourism in France. Includes regional maps. The site is in French.
http://www.pratique.fr/net/tourisme/

Tourisme France: directory of tourist offices; including interactive maps, addresses, hotels, accommodation, museums, sports, etc. (in English and French).
http://www.tourisme.fr

Vegetarian Guide to France: Where to stay and eat in a country known for its love of meat!
http://www.veg.org/veg/Guide/France/index.html

Virtual French Tourist - Links to lots of tourist information including 120 cities around France.
http://globegate.utm.edu/french/vftourist/vftourist.france.html

Webfoot's Guide to France: Links pages including information on cities,transport, food, lodging, history, language and culture, museums, sport, tips for tourists and more
http://www.webfoot.com/travel/guides/france/france.html

 Culture

Bibliothèque Nationale de France - France's new electronic library. http://www.bnf.fr

Cultural Explorer: Join the Eiffel cybership and cruise French Culture in English.
http://ottawa.ambafrance.org/index_eng.html

Cybermax: Student server for France; information about night clubbing, meetings, sports events, exchanges between students. (The site is in French). http://www.cybermax.fr/

Délégation générale à la langue française: Site of the French Ministry of Culture, promoting the French language.
http://www.culture.fr/culture/dglf/garde.htm

France and Francophonie
http://fllc.smu.edu/languages/French.html

The Virtual Baguette: a French/English multimedia on-line
magazine dealing with issues in the French culture.
http://www.mmania.com/

 Miscellaneous

AlaPage - On-line French bookshop listing all titles printed in
France. Also sells CDs and videos. http://www.alapage.com/

Bien-dire, the quarterly journal from France for adult learners
of French. Improve your French and keep in touch with what's
happening in France.   http://www.biendire.com

Frogmag - the electronic magazine of the French community
abroad. Written by its readers, Frogmag aims at publishing
quality articles on any potentially interesting subject.
http://www.princeton.edu/Frogmag/

Le Monde - http://www.lemonde.fr

Libération - http://www.liberation.fr

Ministère des Affaires Etrangères (French Foreign Office)
http://www.france.diplomatie.fr

Novalis - Another on-line French bookstore
http://www.novalis.fr

Outils Multimedia pour l'Enseignement du Français -
Database of multimedia material available for teaching
French as a foreign language.
http://www.france.diplomatie.fr/frmonde/languef/outils/
index.html

RICE - Registered International Correspondents for
Exporting: International business club aiming to develop new
business opportunities between French and foreign
companies. http://www.cci-oise.fr/rice/index.html

AU PAIR WORK

One of the ideal ways to learn a language is, of course, to be surrounded all day long by native speakers. Au pairing allows the visitor to do this, and provides a cheap way of staying in the country for those on a tight budget.

 Au pairs in France receive:

- Around 1650 FF to 1700 FF pocket money per month.
- Accommodation (usually your own bedroom in the house).
- All meals.
- One day off per week (must include a Sunday at least once a month).

Plus those staying in Paris tend to receive the monthly travel card, 'la carte orange'.

As an au pair, you must also be left with enough free time to attend a language course. It is highly recommended that you do so, for not only will it improve your French, but you will invariably meet other au pairs with whom you can discuss your work problems! (NB: Language courses are compulsory for non-EU citizens.)

 In return, au pairs are expected to:

- Look after the children and do light housework (ironing, vacuuming etc.) for about 5 hours per day, 30 hours per week.
- Baby-sit for about two nights per week.

Alternatively, some families are prepared to accept around 10 to 12 hours a week baby-sitting in exchange for a room only. This is a good option if you want to attend a more intensive language course, or if you don't think you can cope with looking after children all day long!

 Conditions:

The au pair must be:

- Single (either male or female, though women are usually prefered)
- Aged 18 to 30 years old
- Prepared to stay for at least three months (the typical au pair stays for one academic year. Maximum stay is 18 months).

 Paperwork:

Au pairs <u>outside</u> the EU (e.g. Americans & Australians) must obtain a *'visa de long séjour'* as a *'stagiaire aide familiale'* from their nearest French consulate. They must do this <u>before arriving in France,</u> as it is not possible to enter on a standard tourist visa and then change to a long stay one.

To obtain this visa, the au pair will need a work agreement approved by the French Ministry of Labour and signed by the family and themselves. An enrolment certificate (*certificat d'inscription*) from a French language school is also required. (Your French family / au pair agency will help you with these papers.)

Au pairs from the EU do not require a long stay visa and can find a family after their arrival in France.

Once in France, the family should declare the au pair as a *'stagiaire aide familiale'* to the French social security office (U.R.S.S.A.F.) and pay the monthly social security contributions.

Applying to agencies / families:

To find a family in France, contact either a local au pair agency in your own country, or go directly to one in France. Whilst EU nationals can wait until their arrival in France to find a position, non-EU nationals must do so before leaving their country.

Au pair agencies will expect you to complete a questionnaire about yourself. Questions are typically about your interests, experience with children, past employment / education, knowledge of French, occupation of your parents, your religion, nationality, whether you can cook, drive, swim etc..

They will also want a reference from someone who knows you, such as a teacher or employer and a letter in French introducing yourself to the family. (Most families expect you to have a basic knowledge of French.)

Please note that French agencies usually charge for their services, so contact several of them to compare their terms. A list of agencies can be found on the following page.

Apart from agencies, a source of vacant positions is the American Church in Paris (65 Quai d' Orsay in the 7th arrondissement). It has a notice board packed with families looking for anglophone au pairs, so it is worth taking along a pen and a piece of paper plus a phone card so that you can call to arrange an interview. (It is wise, however, to let a friend know where you are going, just as a precaution.)

The English Church (rue d' Aguessau) also has a small notice board, which is worth visiting if you don't have any luck at the American Church.

Accueil Familial des Jeunes Etrangers
23, rue du Cherche-Midi, 75006 Paris
Tel: 01 42 22 50 34 Fax: 01 45 44 60 48

Accueil International
2 rue Ducastel, 78100 St-Germain-en-Laye
Tel: 01 39 73 04 98 Fax: 01 39 73 15 25
E-Mail: au-pair@easynet.fr

Amicale Culturelle Internationale
27, rue Godot de Mauroy, 75009 Paris
Tel: 01 47 42 94 21 Fax: 01 49 24 02 67

L'Arche
7, rue Bargue, 75015 Paris.
Tel: 01 42 73 34 39

A.P.E.C. *(Association pour la Promotion des Echanges Culturels)*
11, rue Tronchet, 75008 Paris
Tel: 01 42 68 17 02 Fax: 01 42 68 17 09
E-Mail: apec@imaginet.fr

Association Famille et Jeunesse
4 rue Massena, 06000 Nice
Tel: 04 93 82 28 22 Fax: 04 93 88 12 86
E-mail: Domenge@webstore.fr

Butterfly et Papillon
5 avenue de Genève, 74000 Annecy
Tel: 04 50 46 08 33 Fax: 04 50 67 03 51
E-Mail: aupair.France@wanadoo.fr

Centre d'Echanges Internationaux/Club des 4 Vents
1 rue Gozlin, 75006 Paris
Tel: 01 43 54 85 37 Fax: 01 43 29 06 21
E-Mail: CEIC4V-etudiants@compuserve.com

ECL Toulouse
B.P 214, 31180 Castelmaurou
Tel: 05 61 09 58 81 Fax: 05 61 09 58 81
E-Mail: ecltoulouse@wanadoo.fr

Euro Pair Services
13 Rue Vavin, 75006 Paris
Tel: 01 43 29 80 01 Fax: 01 43 29 80 37

Euromaman
16, rue de la Garenne, 78350 Les Loges en Josas
Tel: 01 39 56 12 30 Fax: 01 39 56 66 44
E-Mail: roussel@maman.com

Goelangues
33 rue de Trevise, 75009 Paris
Tel: 01 45 23 39 39 Fax: 01 45 23 39 23
E-Mail: goelangues@aol.com

Good Morning Europe
38 Rue Traversière, 75012 Paris
Tel: 01 44 87 01 22 Fax: 01 44 87 01 42
E-Mail: au.pair.in.paris@worldnet.fr

Mary Poppins
4 Place de la Fontaine, 38120 Le Fontanil (Grenoble)
Tel: 04 76 75 57 33 Fax: 04 76 75 57 42
E-Mail: Mary.Poppins@wanadoo.fr

Oliver Twist Association
50, ave de la Californie, 33600 Pessac
Tel: 05 57 26 93 26 Fax: 05 56 36 21 85
E-Mail: oliver.twist@wanadoo.fr

Relations Internationales
20, rue de l' Exposition, 75007 Paris.
Tel: 01 45 50 23 23

Séjours Internationaux Linguistiques et Culturels (SILC)
32 Rempart de l'Est, 16022 Angouleme Cédex
Tel: 05 45 97 41 00 Fax: 05 45 95 41 10
E-Mail: contact@silc.asso.fr

Soames Paris Nannies
6, Route de Marlotte, 77690 Montigny sur Loing
Tel: 01 64 78 37 98 Fax: 01 64 45 91 75
E-Mail: Soames.Parisnannies@wanadoo.fr

TILC Au Pair
5 Rue de la Martiniore, 69001 Lyon
Tel: 04 78 28 67 67 Fax: 04 72 07 96 62

USEFUL INFORMATION AND ADDRESSES

EU INITIATIVES FOR STUDENTS, TEACHERS AND SCHOOLS

Further details on all the initiatives listed below can be obtained by calling the numbers shown or by writing to the:

Central Bureau for Educational Visits and Exchanges, 10 Spring Gardens, London SW1A 2BN (U.K.)

 Services Available to Students

Charles de Gaulle Bursary Scheme

- Students aged 17 to 19 years old with a reasonable standard of French can spend a month in France working on a project of their choice.
- Bursaries of up to £800 are available to carry out the student's project or study programme.
- Applications should be made by 31st January of each year and students should expect to be interviewed in March.

For further details call: 0171 389 4930

English Language Assistants Programme

- Generally aimed at undergraduates who need to spend a year in France as part of their course. (Recent graduates are also considered.)
- Students teach English in a French school or college for one academic year.
- Students will have enough time for private study and will also be paid.

- Applications should arrive by 1st December of the year prior to the placement.

For further details call: 0171 389 4764 (England & Wales), 0131 447 8024 (Scotland), 01232 664418 (Northern Ireland)

Lingua Assistant programme

- Part of the EU Socrates programme.
- Aimed at student teachers or students intending to teach as a career.
- Assistants teach English in a school or college in France (or another EU or EEA country).
- Placements last from 3 to 8 months between October and May.
- Assistants receive an allowance.
- Applications should arrive by 1st February each year.

For further details call: 0171 389 4596 (England & Wales), 0131 447 8024 (Scotland) or 01232 664418 (Northern Ireland)

IAESTE (International Association for the Exchange of Students for Technical Experience)

- Aimed at degree level students studying science, technology, engineering or related fields.
- Students undertake work related to their degree in a French company (or one of 60 other member countries on the scheme).
- Students have to pay their own travel costs but are paid a salary by their employers.
- Placements usually last for up to 3 months during the summer, although longer placements at other times in the year are available.
- Applications should arrive during the autumn term.

For further details call: 0171 389 4774 (England, Scotland & Wales) 01232 664418 (Northern Ireland)

LEONARDO da Vinci Programme

- Aims to help students undertake part of their initial vocational training in France (or another EU or EEA member state) through placements and exchanges.
- Colleges or employers, rather than individuals, should apply (various dates throughout the year).

For further details call: 0171 389 4389

 <u>Services Aimed at Schools and Teachers</u>

Teacher Exchange within Europe

- Aimed at full-time modern language teachers working in secondary or further education.
- Teachers exchange jobs for 3 weeks to 1 year with their French counterparts (or German, Austrian, Spanish or Swiss).
- Exchanges can last for up to one year.
- Teachers receive their full salary plus tax relief.
- Applications should be made by mid February each year.

For further details call: 0171 389 4665 (England & Wales), 0131 447 8024 (Scotland) or 01232 664418 (Northern Ireland)

Professional Development Courses: Modern Languages

- Aimed at modern language teachers in secondary, further or adult education.
- Courses last for 2 weeks in France (or Spain, Germany and Italy).
- The programme covers language and contemporary life, with lectures, group work and projects aimed at developing the curriculum.
- Courses are usually during Easter, summer or half-term holidays.

- All costs are met and Lingua grants contribute to accommodation, travel and supply expenses.
- Applications should be made by various deadlines during the year.

For further details call: 0171 389 4665 (England, Scotland and Wales) or 01232 664418 (Northern Ireland)

School and Class Linking

- Service to help either primary or secondary schools find a partner in France (or other countries).
- Once a partner has been found, schools can exchange correspondence, work and visits.
- Applications can be made at any time of year.

For further details call: 0171 389 4419 (England & Wales) 0131 447 8024 (Scotland) 01232 664418 (Northern Ireland)

School Linking Visits

- Short trips designed to help English & Welsh schools form partnerships with schools in France (or other countries), or to develop their existing links with schools.
- Open to teachers and head-teachers at all levels.
- Funds of up to £450 are available to meet travel and other costs.
- Applications should be made at least 6 weeks prior to the proposed visit.

For further details call: 0171 389 4419

Dialogue 2000

- Exchange programme for students aged 16-18 who have studied French up to GCSE level.
- Students spend 1-3 months in a partner institution in France working on a curriculum-linked project.

- The programme also encourages community projects which could include work experience.
- Applications should be made by 15th November, with results announced in December.

For further details call: 0171 389 4159 (England & Wales) 0131 447 8024 (Scotland) 01232 664418 (Northern Ireland)

Lefèvre Trust

- Bursaries of up to £5,000 are available for exchange visits for state secondary schools and colleges in the former ILEA boroughs.
- The bursaries must be shared equally with the French partner school.
- Applications made on behalf of disadvantaged children are given priority.
- Schools can apply at any time of year, but at least 2 months in advance of the exchange.

For further details call: 0171 389 4751

Vocational Training Links

Partner finding service for institutions of further and higher education, training organisations or companies seeking links in France, or other European countries.
Applications can be made at any time of year.

For further details call: 0171 389 4581 (England & Wales) 0131 447 8024 (Scotland) 01232 664418 (Northern Ireland)

COUNCIL ON INTERNATIONAL
EDUCATIONAL EXCHANGE (CIEE)

Organises work experience, study abroad and internships for foreign students in France (and other countries). Also runs the, "Work in France Program", for American students. The maximum stay is 3 months and students require an intermediate level of French. For further details, contact your nearest Council office:

EUROPE

European Headquarters

1 Place de l'Odéon, 75006 Paris
Tel: 33 1 44 41 74 74
Fax: 33 1 43 26 97 45
Email: InfoEurope@ciee.org
or infofrance@ciee.org

Britain
28a Poland Street, London, W1V 3DB
European Information:
Tel: 0171 287 3337
Worldwide Information:
Tel: 0171 437 7767

France
16, rue de Vaugirard, 75006 Paris
Tel: 01 44 41 89 89
Fax: 01 40 51 89 12

12, rue Victor-Leydet
13100 Aix-en-Provence
Tel: 04 42 38 58 82
Fax: 04 42 38 94 00

35, rue Victor-Hugo, 69002 Lyon
Tel: 04 78 38 78 38
Fax: 04 78 38 78 30

Germany

Graf Adolf Str. 64, 40212 Dusseldorf
Tel: 0211 36 30 30
Email:CouncilTravelDusseldorf@ciee.org

Adalbert Str. 32
80799 Munich
Tel: 089 39.50.22
Email: CouncilTravelMunich@ciee.org

UNITED STATES

Arizona
130 E. University Dr., Suite A
Tempe, AZ 85281
Tel: 602-966-3544

California
2486 Channing Way
Berkeley, CA 94704
Tel: 510-848-8604

University of California, Davis
162 Memorial Union Building
Davis, CA 95616
Tel: 916-752-2285

California State University, Fresno
5280 North Jackson
Fresno, CA 93740-0036
Tel: 209-278-6626

California State University, Fullerton
800 North State College Blvd
Fullerton, CA 92834
Mailing address: PO Box 6828
Tel: 714-278-2157

UCSD Price Center
9500 Gilman Drive
La Jolla, CA 92093-0076
Tel: 619-452-0630

1800 Palo Verde Ave., Suite F
Long Beach, CA 90815
Tel: 310-598-3338

10904 Lindbrook Drive
Los Angeles, CA 90024
Tel: 310-208-3551

18111 Nordhoff Street
Matador Book Complex
Cal State Northridge
Northridge, CA 91330-8331
Tel: 818-882-4692

102 University Ave, Suite C
Palo Alto, CA 94301
Tel: 650-325-3888

54 South Raymond Ave
Pasadena, CA 91105
Tel: 818-793-5595

California State University
at Sacramento
University Union
6000 J Street
Sacramento, CA 95819-6017
Tel: 916-278-4224

953 Garnet Avenue
San Diego, CA 92109
Tel: 619-270-6401

743 Fourth Avenue, 1st Fl
San Diego, CA 92101
Tel: 619-544-9632

530 Bush Street, Ground Floor
San Francisco, CA 94108
Tel: 415-421-3473

919 Irving Street, Suite 102
San Francisco, CA 94122
Tel: 415-566-6222

903 Embarcadero del Norte
Santa Barbara, CA 93117
Tel: 805-562-8080

Colorado
1138 13th Street
Boulder, CO 80302
Tel: 303-447-8101

University Memorial Center
Room 164, Campus box 207
University of Colorado
Boulder, CO 80309
Tel: 303-444-3232

900 Auraria Parkway
Tivoli Building
Denver, CO 80204
Tel: 303-571-0630

Connecticut
320 Elm Street
New Haven, CT 06511
Tel: 203-562-5335

District of Columbia
3301 M Street, NW
Washington, DC 20007
Tel: 202-337-6464

Florida
One Datran Center, Suite 220
9100 S. Dadeland Blvd.
Miami, FL 33156
Tel: 305-670-9261

Georgia
Emory Village
1561 N. Decatur Road
Atlanta, GA 30307
Tel: 404-377-9997

Illinois
1634 Orrington Avenue
Evanston, IL 60201
Tel: 847 475 5070

1153 N. Dearborn St., 2nd Fl.
Chicago, IL 60610
Tel: 312-951-0585

Indiana
409 East 4th Street
Bloomington, IN 47408
Tel: 812-330-1600

Iowa
2526 Lincoln Way
Ames, IA50014
Tel: 515-296-2326

Kansas
622 West 12th St
Lawrence, KS 66044
Tel: 913-749-3900

Louisiana
Joseph A. Danna Center
Loyola University
6363 St. Charles Avenue
New Orleans, LA 70118
Tel: 504-866-1767

Maryland
Johns Hopkins University
Gilman Hall Lower Level
3400 North Charles Street
Baltimore, MD 21218
Tel: 410-516-0560

7401 Baltimore Ave
College Park, MD 20740
Tel: 301-779-1172

Massachusetts
44 Main St.
Amherst, MA 01002
Tel: 413-256-1261

273 Newbury St
Boston, MA 02116
Tel: 617-266-1926

12 Eliot St., 2nd Fl.
Harvard Square
Cambridge, MA 02138
Tel: 617-497-1497

Stratton Student Center
M.I.T. W20-024
84 Massachusetts Avenue
Cambridge, MA 02139
Tel: 617-225-2555

Michigan
1218 S. University Drive
Ann Arbor, MI 48104
Tel: 734-998-0200

Michigan State University
MSU Union 106
East Lansing, MI 48824
Tel: 517-432-7722

Minnesota
1501 University Avenue, S.E.
Room 300
Minneapolis, MN 55414
Tel: 612-379-2323

New Jersey
Kilmer Square
86 Albany St
New Brunswick, NJ 08901
Tel: 732-249-6667

New York
206 B Dryden Road
Ithaca, NY 14850
Tel: 607-277-0373

205 East 42nd Street
New York, NY 10017-5706
Tel: 212-822-2700

New York Student Center
895 Amsterdam Avenue
New York, NY 10025
Tel: 212-666-4177

254 Greene Street
New York, NY 10003
Tel: 212-254-2525

North Carolina
137 E. Franklin Street
Suite 106
Chapel Hill, NC 27514
Tel: 919-942-2334

Ohio
8 East 13th Avenue
Columbus, OH 43201
Tel: 614-294-8696

Oregon
877 1/2 East 13th Street
Eugene, OR 97401
Tel: 541-344-2263

University of Oregon
EMU Building
1222 East 13th Street
Eugene, OR 97403
Mailing address: PO Box 3286
Tel: 541-346-5535

1430 SW Park Avenue
Portland, OR 97201
Tel: 503-228-1900

Pennsylvania
931 Harrisburg Avenue
Lancaster, PA 17603
Tel: 717-392-8272

3606 Chestnut Street
Philadelphia, PA 19104
Tel: 215-382-0343

118 Meyran Avenue
Pittsburgh, PA 15213
Tel: 412-683-1881

220 Calder Way
State College, PA 16801
Tel: 814-861-3232

Rhode Island
220 Thayer Street
Providence, RI 02906
Tel: 401-331-5810

Tennessee
125 University Center
University of Tennessee
1502 Cumberland Ave
Knoxville, TN 37916
Tel: 423-974-9200

Texas
2000 Guadalupe Street
Austin, TX 78705
Tel: 512-472-4931

6715 Hillcrest
Dallas, TX 75205
Tel: 214-363-9941

4800 Calhoun St
University Center, Room 32-D
University of Houston
Houston, TX 77204
Tel: 713-743-2777

Utah
1310 East 200 South
Salt Lake City, UT 84102
Tel: 801-582-5840

Washington
1314 N.E. 43rd Street
Suite 210
Seattle, WA 98105
Tel: 206-632-2448

424 Broadway Ave East
Seattle, WA 98102
Tel: 206-329-4567

Wisconsin
429 State St.
Madison, WI 53703
Tel: 608-280-8906

Alternatively, in the US call: 1-800-
2COUNCIL (1-800-226-8624)

REST OF WORLD

Japan
 Cosmos Aoyama, Gallery Floor
5-53-67 Jingumae
Shibuya-ku, Tokyo 150
Tel: 3 5467-5535
Fax: 3 5467-7031

Singapore
110-D Killiney Road
Tai Wah Building
Singapore 0923
Tel: 65 7387-066

Thailand
108/12-13 Kaosan Road
Banglumpoo
Tel: 66 2-282-7705

USEFUL ADDRESSES IN THE U.K.

The French Tourist Office (Maison de la France)
178 Piccadilly, London W1V 0AL TEL: 0891 244123
Open Monday to Friday 9am to 5pm *(Calls charged at 39p per minute off peak, 49p at all other times.)*

Institut Français - Cultural Centre
17 Queensberry Place, London SW7 2DT
TEL: 0171 838 2144 FAX: 0171 838 2145
Library with audio books, Cds, CD-ROMs, comic strips, etc.
Also organises exhibitions, lectures, film shows and French tuition
'à la carte'.

Institut Français - Language Centre
14 Cromwell Road, London SW7 2JR
TEL: 0171 581 2701 FAX: 0171 581 2910

Institut Français - Children's Library
32 Harrington Road, London SW7 2DT   TEL: 0171 838 2157

Booksellers:

The European Bookshop
5 Warwick Street, London W1R 5RA
TEL: 0171 734 5259 FAX: 0171 287 1720

France (Canterbury)
29-30 Palace Street, Canterbury CT1 2DZ
TEL: 01227 454508 FAX: 01227 762078

France Magasin
France House, Digbeth Street, Stow-on-the-Wold, Glos. GL54 1BN
TEL: 01451 870920 FAX: 01451 831367
Books, maps, guides etc.

The French Bookshop (UK) Ltd.
28, Bute Street, South Kensington, London SW7 3EX
TEL: 0171 584 2840 FAX: 0171 823 9259

The French Booksellers - Librairie La Page
7, Harrington Road, London SW7. TEL: 0171 589 5991

The French Theatre Bookshop
52, Fitzroy Street, London W1P 6JR
TEL: 0171 387 9373 FAX: 0171 387 2161

Grant and Cutler Ltd
55-57 Great Marlborough Street, London W1V 2AY
TEL: 0171 734 2012 FAX: 0171 734 9272

LCL International Booksellers Ltd
104 Judd Street, London WC1H 9NT
TEL: 0171 837 0487 FAX: 0171 833 9452

Stanfords
12-14 Long Acre, Covent Garden, London WC2E 9LP
TEL: 0171 836 132
Large selection of maps and guides.

The Travel Bookshop
13 Blenheim Crescent, London W11 2EE
TEL: 0171 229 5260 FAX: 0171 243 1552
Hundreds of travel books on France, including out-of-print titles.

Language Travel Agents / Organisations:

The following organisations place groups / individuals in language
courses throughout France. They usually take care of all the travel
arrangements and can find accommodation as well.

Auto Focus
32 Florence Letek, 32 Elmtree Greetn, Great Missenden
Buckinghamshire HP16 9AF TEL/ FAX: 01494 864933
- Organises homestays.

The Cambridge Advisory Service
Rectory Lane, Kingston, Cambridge CB3 7NL
TEL: 01223 264089 FAX: 01223 704720

Centre d' Echanges Internationaux (CEI)
16 Leicester Square, London WC2H 7NH
TEL: 0171 734 0733 FAX: 0171 734 1357

CESA Languages Abroad
Western House, Malpas, Truro TR1 1SQ
TEL: 01872 225300 FAX: 01872 225400
languages@cesa.demon.co.uk

Challenge Educational Services Ltd.
101 Lorna Road, Hove, East Sussex BN3 3EL
TEL: 01273 220261 FAX: 01273 220376

En-Famille Overseas
The Old Stables, 60b Maltravers Street, Arundel,
West Sussex BN18 9BG
TEL: 01903 883266 FAX: 01903 883582

International Links
145 Manygate Lane, Shepperton, Middlesex TW17 9EP
TEL: 01932 229300 FAX: 01932 222294

Interspeak
The Coach House, Blackwood, Lanark ML11 0JG
TEL: 01555 894219 FAX: 01555 894954
- *specialises in work placements.*

Schools into Europe
'Cesail-y-Bryn', Wenallt Road, Rhiwbina, Cardiff. CF4 6TQ
TEL: 01222 522236 / 7 FAX: 01222 520027

See Europe Ltd.
1 Church Walk Studios, Beales Lane, Weybridge, Surrey. KT13 8JS
TEL: 01932 840440 FAX: 01932 856514

SIBS
West Wing, Fen Drayton House, Fen Drayton, Cambridge CB4 5SW
TEL : 01954 231956 FAX: 01954 232294

 USEFUL ADDRESSES IN FRANCE

Language Travel Agents / Organisations:

ACTE - International
39, rue du Sahel, 75012 Paris
Tel: 01 43 42 48 84 Fax: 01 43 41 51 17
Email: acte_int@mail.club-internet.fr
Places students in language schools and universities around France. Can also arrange Easter and summer courses for 14-18 year olds, with host-family accommodation.

APM - Option Vacances
13, rue Sainte Cécile, 75009 Paris
Tel: 01 53 24 90 90 Fax: 01 53 24 90 91
Email: APMOVJ@aol.com
Various programmes including language courses, sports, artistic courses etc. 8 centres around France, for ages 4-25 years.

Association Contacts
3, rue Maréchal Foch, 37000 Tours
Tel: 02 47 20 20 57 Fax: 02 47 20 68 92
Organises linguistic and cultural programmes around France for groups or individuals aged 12-18.
Can also arrange home-stay courses, au-pair programmes and training programmes with companies.

BEC Séjours Linguistiques
5, rue Richepanse, 75008 Paris
Tel: 01 42 60 35 57 Fax: 01 42 60 36 55
Places students in language schools around France. Also arranges 1-1 tuition and host-family accommodation.

Cap Monde
11, quai Conti, 78430 Louveciennes
Tel: 01 30 82 15 15 Fax: 01 30 82 22 22
Specialises in providing school groups with language, sporting or cultural trips. Has over 40 centres and arranges accommodation for the group.

CEI / Club des Quatre Vents
BP 5, 75660 Paris Cedex 14
Tel: 01 45 65 95 21 Fax: 01 45 65 95 30
Email: CEI_4Vents@compuserve.com
Arranges summer language courses for young people. Also, summer camps with French youths, company training programmes and specialist courses (art lovers, cookery etc.).

CLC - Club Langues et Civilisations
rue de la Comtesse Cécile, 12000 Rodez
Tel: 05 65 77 50 13 Fax: 05 65 42 84 57
Email: clc.contact@inforsud.fr
Arranges language programmes around France. Intensive courses, home-stay, au-pair programmes and language + tennis courses. Also tailor-made programmes for groups, including 3-4 day mini-breaks.

Comité d'Accueil
21, rue St.Fargeau, BP 313, 75989 Paris Cedex 20
Tel: 01 43 58 95 28 Fax: 01 43 58 95 08
Organises group holidays for adolescents and finds accommodation for groups throughout France in schools, colleges etc.

Envol Espace
Le Trifide, rue Claude-Bloch, 14050 Caen Cedex
Tel: 02 31 43 82 83 Fax: 02 31 43 81 31
Tour operator offering language programmes, cultural and pedagogical trips, accommodation with families, hostels or hotels.

OTU Voyage
151, Avenue Ledru-Rollin, 75011 Paris
Tel: 01 43 79 07 95 Fax: 01 43 79 07 85
Email: otuvoyage@terranet.fr
Large student travel agency. As well as budget accommodation, it can also book language courses, sell ISIC cards, arrange car rental etc.

SILC (Séjours Internationaux Linguistiques et Culturels)
32, rempart de l'Est, 16022 Angoulême Cedex
Tel: 05 45 97 41 00 Fax: 05 45 95 41 10
Email: contact@silc.asso.fr
(UK Office: Hartcran House, suite 9, Carpenders Park, Watford. WD1 5BE. Tel: 0181 421 3333 Fax: 0181 421 2777
Email: silcuk@btinternet.com)
Arranges language courses, 1-1 tuition, high school & university admittance and au-pair programmes. 11 regional offices and a language school in Paris.

SOUFFLE
BP 133, 83957 La Garde Cedex
Tel: 04 94 21 20 92 Fax: 04 94 21 22 17
Email: souffle@toulon.pacwan.net
Organisation representing 18 French language schools.

UNOSEL -
Union Nationale des Organisations de Séjours Linguistiques
15-19, rue des Mathurins, 75009 Paris
Tel: 01 49 24 03 61 Fax: 01 42 65 39 38
Organisation which represents 40 schools around France.

Vacances pour Tous
21, rue Saint-Fargeau, BP 313, 75989 Paris Cedex 20
Tel: 01 43 58 95 74 Fax: 01 43 58 95 08
Email: vacances-ligue@ligue.cie.fr
*The vacations department of the "Ligue Française de
l'Enseignement"- the French Teaching League. Organises general
holiday packages for children, adolescents and young adults. Also
runs educational school tours and language programmes.*

Youth Information Centres
*Can supply information on temporary work, accommodation, leisure
activities etc.*

Paris:
Centre d'Information et Documentation de la Jeunesse (CIDJ)
101, quai Branly, 75740 Paris Tel: 01 44 49 12 00

Regional:
CRIJ Ain-Loire-Rhône - 9, quai des Célestins, 69216 Lyon cedex 02
Tel: 04 72 77 00 66
CRIJ Alpes - Vivarais - 8, rue Voltaire, 38000 Grenoble.
Tel: 04 76 54 70 38
CRIJ Alsace - 7, rue des Ecrivains, 67000 Strasbourg.
Tel: 03 88 37 33 33
CRIJ Aquitaine - 5, rue Duffour Dubergier and 125, cours Alsace-Lorraine,
33000 Bordeaux. Tel: 05 56 56 10 56
CRIJ Auvergne - 5, roe Saint-Genès, 63000 Clermont-Ferrand.
Tel: 04 73 92 30 50
CRIJ Burgundy - 18, rue Audra, 21000 Dijon Tel: 03 80 44 18 45
CRIJ Brittany - Maison du Champ de Mars, 6 cours des Alliés,
35043 Rennes cedex Tel: 02 99 31 47 48
CRIJ Centre - 3-5, boulevard de Verdun, 45000 Orléans.
Tel: 02 38 78 91 78
CRIJ Champagne-Ardennes - 41, rue de Talleyrand, 51100 Reims
Tel: 03 26 47 46 70
CRIJ Corsica - 3, boulevard Auguste-Gaudin, 20294 Bastia cedex.
Tel: 04 95 32 50 77
CRIJ Côte d'Azur - 19, rue Gioffrédo, 06000 Nice. Tel: 04 93 80 93 93
CRIJ Franche-Comté - 27, rue de la République , 25000 Besançon.
Tel: 03 81 21 16 16
CRIJ Haute-Normandie - 84, rue Beauvoisine, 76000 Rouen.
Tel: 02 35 98 38 75
CRIJ Limousin - 27, boulevard de la Corderie, 87031 Limoges cedex
Tel: 05 55 45 18 70
CRIJ Lorraine - 20, quai Claude-le-Lorrain, 54000 Nancy.
Tel: 03 83 37 04 46

CRIJ Lower-Normandy - 16, rue Neuve-Saint-Jean, 14000 Caen.
Tel: 02 31 85 73 60
CRIJ Midi-Pyrenees - 17, rue de Metz, 31000 Toulouse.
Tel: 05 61 21 20 20
CRIJ Nord-Pas-de-Calais - 2, rue Nicolas Leblanc, 59000 Lille.
Tel: 03 20 12 87 30
CRIJ Pays de la Loire - 28, rue du Calvaire, 44000 Nantes.
Tel: 02 51 72 94 50
CRIJ Picardy - 56, rue du Vivier, 80000 Amiens. Tel: 03 22 71 16 26
CRIJ Poitou-Charentes - 64, rue Gambetta, 86000 Poitiers.
Tel: 05 49 60 68 68

CNOUS : Main office: 69, quai d'Orsay, 75007 Paris. Tel: 01 44 18 53 00

Other useful addresses in France:

Office de tourisme et syndicats d'initiative (French tourist office)
280, boulevard St. Germain, 75007 Paris. TEL: 01 44 11 10 30

Office de tourisme de Paris (Paris tourist office)
127, avenue des Champs-Elysées, 75008 Paris
TEL: 01 49 52 53 54 FAX: 01 49 52 53 00 TELEX: 645 439
Information: 01 49 52 53 55

AJF - Accueil des Jeunes en France   (for individuals)
119, rue Saint -Martin, 75004 Paris
TEL: 01 42 77 87 80 FAX: 01 42 77 70 48
Central reservation office specialising in holidays for young people.

AJF - Accueil des Jeunes en France (for groups)
151, avenue Ledru-Rollin, 75011 Paris
TEL: 01 43 79 53 86 FAX: 01 43 79 35 63
As above, but for group travel.

Bien-dire
9, rue J. Soulary, 69004 Lyon.   FAX: 04 78 30 87 03
*Quarterly journal for adult learners of French. Available with or
without audio cassettes, this is a well researched and interesting
publication.*

BVJ (Bureau des Voyages de la Jeunesse)
20, rue Jean-Jacques Rousseau, 75001 Paris
TEL: 01 42 36 88 18 FAX: 01 42 33 40 53
Tourist association for young people.

How to improve your French

Bien-dire makes learning French an enjoyable and stimulating experience. It's a quarterly journal specially written and designed for adult learners of French.

You will keep in touch with what's happening in France whilst improving your vocabulary, fluency and confidence.

Key words and expressions are high-lighted and listed with an English translation.

We help you improve pronunciation and comprehension too with the tapes or CDs of selected articles.

You can subscribe to *Bien-dire* for only £23 a year. Just £11 more gives you the audio cassettes too. Postage within Europe is included.

Fax or mail Subscription Application and we'll send your first issue by return.

Subscription Application
1 year subscription (4 issues) :
- ❑ Journal only   199 FF (£23 / US$ 39)
- ❑ Journal + tape   299 FF (£34 / US$ 58)
- ❑ Journal + CD   549 FF (£59 / US$ 99)
Subscribers outside Europe add: 65 FF (US$ 11)

Dr/ Mr/ Mrs/ Ms: _____

Address: _____

Post code: _____ Country: _____

I wish to pay by credit card - Visa / Mastercard:
N°: _____
                                    Signature:
expiry date: _____

Payments by credit cards will be debited in French Francs
Cheques (£ / US$ / FF) are payable to Bien-dire

Fax: **+33 (0) 4 78 30 87 03**   *Bien-dire* (EP)
Visit our web site: **9 rue J. Soulary**
http://www.biendire.com   **69004 LYON**
journal@biendire.com   **FRANCE**

French Tourist Offices Overseas (Maison de la France):

Australia:
25 Bligh Street, Sydney NSW 2000
TEL: (02) 92 31 52 44
FAX: (02) 92 21 86 82
E-Mail: french@ozemail.com

Canada:
1981 Avenue McGill College
Suite 490, Montreal H3A 2W9
TEL: (514) 288 4264
FAX: (514) 845 4868

30 St. Patrick Street
Suite 700, Toronto M5T 3A3
TEL: (416) 593 4723
FAX: (416) 979 7587

Ireland:
35 Lower Abbey Street, Dublin 1
TEL: (01) 703 4046
FAX: (01) 874 7324

South Africa:
196 Oxford Road, Oxford Manor
Illovo 2196
TEL: (011) 880 8062
FAX: (011) 880 7772

United States:
444 Madison Avenue, 16th Floor
New York NY 10022
TEL: 900 990 0040
FAX: (212) 838 7855

9454 Wilshire Blvd - Suite 715
Beverly Hills. CA 90212-2967
TEL: (310) 271 6665
FAX: (310) 276 2835

676 North Michigan Avenue,
Suite 3360. Chicago, Illinois 60611-2819
TEL: (312) 751 7800
FAX: (312) 337 6339

METRIC CONVERSION TABLES

The central figures represent either of the two adjacent columns.
(eg. 1 mile = 1.609 kilometre and 1 kilometre = 0.621 miles)

Kilometres		Miles	Kilograms		Pounds
1.609	1	0.621	0.113	¼	0.551
8.047	5	3.107	0.454	1	2.205
16.093	10	6.214	2.268	5	11.023

Metres		Yards	Litres		Pints
0.914	1	1.094	0.284	½	0.880
4.572	5	5.468	0.568	1	1.760
9.144	10	10.936	2.841	5	8.800

Centimetres		Inches	Litres		Gallons
2.540	1	0.394	4.546	1	0.220
12.700	5	1.969	22.730	5	1.100
27.940	11	4.331	45.460	10	2.200

INTERNATIONAL CLOTHING SIZES

Please note that all size equivalents are approximate.

Women: Shoes
British	4½	5	51½	6	6½	7
European	38	38	39	39	40	41
American	6	6½	7	7½	8	8½

Women: Dresses & Suits
British	8	10	12	14	16	18
European	36	38	40	42	44	46
American	6	8	10	12	14	16

Men: Shoes
British	7	7½	8½	9½	10½	11
European	41	42	43	44	45	46
American	8	8½	9½	10½	11½	12

Men: Suits & Coats
British	38	40	42	44	46	48
European	48	50	52	54	56	58
American	38	40	42	44	46	48

Men: Shirts
British	14½	15	15½	16	16½	17
European	37	38	39	41	42	43
American	14½	15	15½	16	16½	17

Si vous dirigez une école de langue française pour étrangers et que votre établissement n'apparaît pas dans notre livre, n'hésitez pas de nous contacter à l'adresse suivante et nous vous enverrons tous les renseignements nécessaires.

Europa Pages
PO Box 1369
ASCOT
SL5 7YB
England

E-Mail: france@europa-pages.co.uk

Have you been to a language school in France which is not included in this book? Do you have any comments about a course you have attended? If so, please write to us at the above address. We greatly appreciate all the information that is sent to us, and your letters will help to improve our next edition, providing a better service for other language learners.